WORTHY OF WEARING

WORTHY

OF

WEARING

—

NICOLE M. CARUSO

Sophia Institute Press
Box 5284, Manchester, NH 03108
1-800-888-9344

www.SophiaInstitute.com

Sophia Institute Press® is a registered trademark of Sophia Institute.

Library of Congress Cataloging-in-Publication Data

Names: Caruso, Nicole Marie, author.
Title: Worthy of wearing : how personal style expresses our feminine genius / Nicole M. Caruso.
Description: Manchester, New Hampshire : Sophia Institute Press, 2021
Includes bibliographical references.
Identifiers: LCCN 2020055065 | ISBN 9781644133415 (hardcover)
Subjects: LCSH: Fashion. | Women's clothing — Psychological aspects. | Women's clothing — Religious aspects. | Christian women — Clothing. | Feminine beauty (Aesthetics)
Classification: LCC TT507 .C354 2021 | DDC 746.9/2 — dc23
LC record available at https://lccn.loc.gov/2020055065

First Printing

DEDICATION

To my Stephen, this book would not exist without your generous heart, patient fathering, endless encouragement, and late-night strategy sessions. God knew I needed a man like you, and I am so blessed to be your wife.

To my beautiful children, thank you for teaching me about what agape really is. I am so proud to be your mama.

I love you as deep as the ocean.

TABLE

OF

CONTENTS

INTRODUCTION

Let me start by explaining what this book is not. This book is not a manifesto on what is hot and what is not. Do not expect it to be like those magazine articles that tell you the Ten Things Every Woman Should Own. This book won't reveal a set of specific rules that every woman must follow to be stylish. Last of all, this book will not tell you what your style should be; rather, it will teach you how to uncover what is already in your heart, so you can wear a tiny piece of it on your sleeve.

Worthy of Wearing is a mindset, a thought process that reminds us (including me) that we are precious in God's eyes and that we are worthy of wearing the things that make us feel beautiful. We owe it to ourselves to dress in what fills us with joy, suits our body, and matches our vocation and lifestyle. That colorful top you love that hangs in the back of your closet, to be worn "another day"? Why not today? The perfectly tailored pants that make you feel as if you can tackle anything that comes your way? Throw them on! That necklace your grandmother passed down to you that still faintly smells like her perfume? Seize the moment and wear it proudly. When we keep wearing the same old clothes and ignore the beautiful pieces that give us joy, we end up with a closet full of lovely things that never get worn. What a shame!

From my early childhood, I have been delighted by clothing, personal style, makeup, photography, film, and everything in between. My first job was in a luxury jewelry store in my hometown, and I continued to work many retail jobs to earn income, though much of the time it didn't feel like work at all. The little luxury makeup boutique in Westport, Connecticut; the flagship Gap store on 59th Street; and big-time Saks Fifth Avenue—all these places gave me the opportunity to help women of all ages with everything from fitting undergarments, picking designer bags, and nailing the perfect cat eyeliner to selecting diamonds and finding the perfect pair of jeans for their body type. Once I saw a woman's eyes light up and her confidence bubble over, I experienced a need-for-speed adrenaline rush of fulfillment. I couldn't get enough.

Still, I longed for more. I deeply desired to break into my dream industry: fashion. After my husband completed an Air Force assignment in Texas, we moved back to New York City, where we fell in love, so I could pursue my lifelong dream. And it happened (thanks to a best friend, who forwarded my résumé to her friend)! I had my fashion-girl moments as an intern and a temp traipsing through Manhattan showrooms, sitting in on buyer meetings with big-time sales executives, dressing models, dancing at fashion show after-parties, and catching a glimpse of plenty of celebrities. I was given the insider's look at the fashion industry, right in the Garment District of New York, New York. And yes, it was like the movies (even *The Devil Wears Prada* part).

That part of my life was all about the look and the label. I learned how to answer the question "Who is your bag?" as in, "Who is the designer of your bag?" Once I discerned my call to exit the industry, I struggled with getting dressed when it wasn't for someone else to see, even when that "someone else" was just a fellow New Yorker on the sidewalk, participating in the city's people-watching culture. If I wasn't seen by other people, did getting dressed matter?

Do you know who really taught me what Worthy of Wearing means? It wasn't a master seamstress, style forecaster, or trendsetter. It was my daughter, Cecilia. Every morning, she beats me at getting dressed and jumpstarts her day with a twirl in her outfit. At age two, she grabbed my vintage magenta scarf and tied it around her neck. At age three, she wore her Christmas dress every Sunday until it didn't fit anymore, and at age four, she wore a pink sequin dress on our weekly trip to the library. Many of our neighbors would stop and smile at her joy. She never apologized for looking so snazzy; instead, she humbly grinned, shrugged her shoulders, and went on giggling and skipping down the sidewalk.

What this beautiful little soul showed me was that wearing your favorite things makes your heart happy. With pure intentions and a happy heart, we can follow the example of St. Thérèse of Lisieux and do "small things with great love" because our confidence is rooted in Christ. I gave Cecilia's methods a try, and wore my fashion-girl favorites as a stay-at-home mom. Something was lighter. I felt like myself again, rather than feeling as if I were "just a mom." Though I found incredible meaning and fulfillment in mothering my toddler while wearing simple clothing that fulfilled the need of covering my body, I reconnected with my life purpose when I dressed for my day with a little pizzazz. The mix of my "old" life with my new life allowed me to harness a new kind of confidence. Personal style for the sake of being stylish and noticed is muddied with vanity, but personal style for the sake of feeling confident in your God-given purpose and mission is empowering and freeing. Clothing that shares our story and mission and assists us in our work can be worn for the greater glory of God.

When I set out to write this book, I knew I wanted to feature real women in these pages. I wanted to show you the many faces of authentic beauty that God created, and I wanted you to feel swept away by the design. The incredible women featured in this book are my friends and family. They are talented, intelligent, creative, witty, and caring. Above all, they seek to love God with all their heart. When I see their faces as I flip through these pages, I find myself smiling over their magnetic joy. My hope is that this book edifies your femininity and inspires you to celebrate who God made you to be.

Instead of hiring a stylist to bring in gorgeous designer clothing, these friends of mine shopped their closets. Each one is wearing her own clothes (or borrowing mine!), which effortlessly and elegantly express who she is. Thanks to a little hair and makeup, God-given perfect weather, and the keen eye of photographer Marquel Patton, the words of this book can come alive in photos.

Some words of encouragement I have for you: you can do this. You don't need to go to fashion school, hire a stylist, or wear a certain clothing size. It doesn't matter if you live on a farm, in a cul-de-sac, or in a high-rise apartment. And it definitely doesn't matter if you frequent department stores or thrift stores to build your wardrobe. Furthermore, what I love and gravitate toward may be completely different from what inspires you, and I think that is a very, very good thing. You can do this, I promise! Just be patient with yourself and your wallet, and don't give up.

Whether you can't stand your clothes, love your clothes but find them ill-suited for your current phase of life, or are still sorting out what your personal style is, you are not alone. I want to thank you for joining me on this journey and propelling me to finally write this book, which has been on my heart since I was a girl.

Thank you for telling your friends, sisters, roommates, and cousins to join in. Thank you for sending me notes saying you finally dumped that terrible boyfriend, embraced your figure, applied for that new job, or [insert scary but good thing here]. That is how I knew from the get-go that this message was not mine but Christ's. He wants us to know our God-given worth. He has big plans for our lives.

"Yea, the very hairs of your head are all numbered. Fear not therefore: you are of more value than many sparrows."

Luke 12:7
(Douay-Rheims)

Nicole

A
THANK YOU

from Pope St. John Paul II

Thank you, *women who are mothers!* You have sheltered human beings within yourselves in a unique experience of joy and travail. This experience makes you become God's own smile upon the newborn child, the one who guides your child's first steps, who helps it to grow, and who is the anchor as the child makes its way along the journey of life.

Thank you, *women who are wives!* You irrevocably join your future to that of your husbands, in a relationship of mutual giving, at the service of love and life.

Thank you, *women who are daughters and women who are sisters!* Into the heart of the family, and then of all society, you bring the richness of your sensitivity, your intuitiveness, your generosity and fidelity.

Thank you, *women who work!* You are present and active in every area of life — social, economic, cultural, artistic and political. In this way you make an indispensable contribution to the growth of a culture which unites reason and feeling, to a model of life ever open to the sense of "mystery," to the establishment of economic and political structures ever more worthy of humanity.

Thank you, *consecrated women!* Following the example of the greatest of women, the Mother of Jesus Christ, the Incarnate Word, you open yourselves with obedience and fidelity to the gift of God's love. You help the Church and all mankind to experience a "spousal" relationship to God, one which magnificently expresses the fellowship which God wishes to establish with his creatures.

Thank you, *every woman*, for the simple fact of being a woman! Through the insight which is so much a part of your womanhood you enrich the world's understanding and help to make human relations more honest and authentic.

Letter to Women, June 29, 1995

Why We Are
Worthy

CHAPTER I

KNOW
YOU ARE
WORTHY

Know *you are* Worthy

Did you know the Bible reinforces our worth as women? Read Proverbs 31:10, the beginning of the "Poem on the Woman of Worth." The verse says: "Who can find a woman of worth? Far beyond jewels is her value." We can't argue with the living Word of God.

But what does it mean to be worthy? This is something I've wondered with every new phase of my life. During some of those phases, I felt a puzzling disconnect between the person I wanted to be, the person others thought I should be, and the person I saw in the mirror. Confusion and self-doubt clouded my heart. My dreams seemed so distant, and I convinced myself I was unworthy of pursuing them.

WHO CAN FIND A

(WOMAN)

OF WORTH? FAR BEYOND
JEWELS IS HER VALUE.

The biggest lie women believe today is that we are unworthy. We limit ourselves, pause our dreams, and brood in resignation. We settle for the controlling boyfriend. We don't speak up when someone disrespects us. We shrink when our beliefs are challenged, or unfortunately, we succumb to indifference. And worst of all, we pass on the voices of criticism and shame to the people in our sphere of influence: our daughters, friends, cousins, and nieces. As the phrase "hurt people hurt people" reminds us, pain is transferable. Stay with me, and know that I will be with you every step of the way as you discover how to stop the lie that you are unworthy dead in its tracks.

No matter what stage of life you're in, I want you to know that you are worthy of love. You were made in the image and likeness of God. You are a precious daughter of the King of Kings. Your Heavenly Father has counted every hair on your head, and He gazes upon you with tenderness, despite your human frailty. He sees you as you are — imperfect and prone to sin — and still adores you as His "pearl of great price." The Creator of the universe made you to be exactly who you are. Even if you don't feel beautiful, you were made beautiful. I'll say it again: you were made beautiful, and you are beautiful, even if you struggle with confidence, don't know what your personal style is, or feel a bit lost when you get dressed. Let the truth of your God-given beauty mark your heart.

This book is a love letter that you are worthy of wearing what makes you feel beautiful and confident. Did you know that you are worthy of a nice top on a Tuesday, or your favorite shoes on a Friday? Maybe it's 2:00 p.m. and you're having a hard day. Why not spend a few moments in prayer and then put on some lipstick? Take a few deep breaths, and have faith that you can carry on with Christ at your side. Even if you don't feel worthy, you can poke a pinhole in the darkness and spotlight Christ's presence in your life, the way a camera obscura captures light. That pinhole creates space for Christ to enter with His love.

In order to *feel worthy*, you must make a habit of accepting your worth. When I first became a mother in 2014, after four years of trying to conceive, I resigned myself to the servitude of my vocation. There was no room for self-care when I barely had time to shower without my colicky baby crying out or spitting up. I was afraid she would choke if I left her alone for more than two minutes. On a few occasions, she proved me right. Keeping up with the never-ending chores in my home was a losing battle. Nothing ever felt "done" the way it did when I was a working professional or a student. When you're in survival mode, it's impossible to see three feet ahead, let alone plan an elaborate self-care routine or design a wardrobe that perfectly and effortlessly expresses who you are and allows your soul to speak through your garments.

Sadly, many women fall prey to the mind-set that we shouldn't take time for ourselves, whether by maintaining our hygiene, praying, or practicing self-care, because these activities take us away from our duties. Self-care has become a bit of a contemporary mantra and often is devoid of meaning beyond indulgence. We need the *why* behind self-care.

As women, we love to nurture, and we often devote ourselves to nurturing our apostolate, our relationships, and our responsibilities at the expense of our own needs. We acquiesce to the demands of our to-do list, and by neglecting ourselves, we lose sight of who we are, to the point that we don't recognize the person in the mirror.

This is the case not just for mothers but for any woman who prioritizes her tasks over taking care of herself to a fault. Being a workaholic, no matter your vocation, often leads to burnout and resentment of the very people you love and serve. Ultimately, when we neglect our need for self-care, inspiration, friendship, prayer, exercise, and healthy habits, we dim the light of Christ within us. In Luke 11:33, Jesus says, "No one who lights a lamp hides it away or places it [under a bushel basket], but on a lampstand so that those who enter might see the light." He continues in verse 36, "If your whole body is full of light, and no part of it is in darkness, then it will be as full of light as a lamp illuminating you with its brightness." How can we become a light for the world, without hiding away our radiance? Believing in our worth is the first step.

Remember what St. Paul said: "For by grace you have been saved through faith, and this is not from you; it is the gift of God; it is not from works, so no one may boast. For we are his handiwork, created in Christ Jesus for the good works that God has prepared in advance, that we should live in them" (Eph. 2:8–10). No matter what we do or what we have, we are His handiwork: special, unique, and unrepeatable. We must embrace our identity in this way because it flips everything the culture tells us on its head. Have you ever thought that your confidence in who God created you to be could be a gift to share with the world? I'm here to say, you better believe it.

Like many women, I haven't always been confident in who I am. I've struggled with my identity, my mission, and during a summer abroad in Rome, my vocation. Bullies, pop culture, and those gnawing negative voices have tried many times to confuse me, quiet me, and lead me astray. Those negative voices want you to feel small, incapable, unlovable, and burdensome so that you will keep your light hidden. When we surrender to the voices of fear and shame, they saturate our world with emptiness and rob us of our chance to show Christ to others.

So what is the greatest weapon we have against insecurity? Seeing ourselves the way God sees us, loving ourselves the way He loves us, and sharing that love freely. When we allow Christ into our heart, no matter how shattered it is, He heals it. With that healing comes the ability to trust God, accept His love, and become His hands and feet in this world.

The Worthy of Wearing movement, and the pages you now cradle in your hands, were born out of my own need for a mindset shift when

"YOU ALONE

CAN SATISFY THE

LONGINGS THAT

CONSUME US."

✝

ST. GREGORY NAZIANZEN

I completely lost touch with what feeling like myself really meant. So what is Worthy of Wearing, exactly?

Worthy of Wearing is a movement to teach you how to show up for yourself so you can carry out the mission God put on your heart at your Baptism. On that day, He bestowed specific gifts and charisms upon you to help you share His love, His beauty, and His truth with everyone you encounter, even in the simplest ways.

Worthy of Wearing is a mindset that gives you permission to embrace and celebrate your inherent beauty. You are worthy of wearing the things that make you feel beautiful, give you a boost of confidence, and act as reminders that you are a sacred creation of God, made with intention and purpose according to His holy will. When we rediscover our passion, walk with a confident stride, and meet the gaze of those we serve with great love and deep peace, we can change hearts.

Whether you're a student, professional, creative, missionary, mother, caretaker, or an epic combination of all of these, I am going to help you discover your self-worth, translate it to your wardrobe, and help you *"set the world ablaze,"* as St. Catherine of Siena once wrote.

You are worth

You are *worthy* of
wearing
the *things* that
make you feel *beautiful*,
give you a boost of
confidence,
and act as *reminders*
that you are a sacred
creation of God
made with *intention*
and *purpose*
according to His
holy will.

01. What is your earliest memory of feeling beautiful and confident in your own skin?

02. What is one memory you have of questioning your self-worth? Has that wound healed?

03. How many hours a week do you spend...

...caring for your spiritual needs (prayer, adoration, spiritual direction, receiving the sacraments)?

...caring for your body (hygiene, clothing, nutrition, rest)?

...caring for your emotional needs (relationships, journaling, counseling)?

04. When do you feel valued?

05. Who in your life celebrates you for who you are?

06. What is one activity or hobby that makes you realize your worth? (Do that more often!)

07. How can you show up for yourself more each week?

MINDSET CHECK

Many of us struggle to see ourselves with God the Father's loving gaze.
Use this questionnaire to think more deeply on who you are.

08. What is one affirmation you can say each day to remind yourself of your God-given value?

CELEBRATE YOUR FEMININE GENIUS

Celebrate *Your* Feminine *Genius*

"IS THIS TOO MUCH?"

Maybe, like me, you've had that thought before. The moment you've finally found the perfect thing to wear, the negative voice creeps in, saying: "Shame on you for feeling beautiful. So materialistic and vain… You think you're better than everyone else, and you make people feel bad by shining your light with confidence." But nothing could be further from the truth.

I've always loved the phrase "feminine genius," coined by Pope St. John Paul II to describe the mystique of womanhood. In his 1995 *Letter to Women*, he taught that universal dignity — "the state or quality of being worthy of honor or respect," according to the Oxford English Dictionary — is "written in the heart of every human being,"[1] and he celebrated the distinctive call of each woman to safeguard that dignity. He said, "Necessary emphasis should be placed on the 'genius of women,' not only by considering great and famous women of the past or present, but also those ordinary women who reveal the gift of their womanhood by placing themselves at the service of others in their everyday lives."[2]

Pope John Paul II's concept of the feminine genius shows how every woman can "reign" with God through her state in life — namely, by sharing her gifts with others, and especially her heart. Contrary to our culture, which portrays the pursuit of heroic virtue as boring, Pope John Paul II lovingly reminds us that living our mission, whether public or private, great or ordinary, is a gift to this world and an expression of God.

We've all seen the world's image of "strong women" in the media we consume. They are usually sneakily resourceful, bossy, conniving, intimidatingly beautiful, rich, and inordinately thin. They have "the life"; they attend lavish parties, have friends in high places, never miss out on fun, and enjoy successful careers that afford them every luxury they dream of, all while the women and men in their lives secretly fear them. In a word, these women are Barbies.

By contrast, Pope John Paul II recognized the need for women to see their beauty and strength as inherent to their creation in the image and likeness of God. Strength is not a merit that we gain by inspiring fear or by eclipsing our femininity with masculine behavior. In his Letter to Women, Pope John Paul II wrote: "Women's dignity has often been unacknowledged and their prerogatives misrepresented; they have often been relegated to the margins of society and even reduced to servitude. This has prevented women from truly being themselves and it has resulted in a spiritual impoverishment of humanity."[3]

That line really resonates with me. Our purpose is not to be servants whose existence fulfills an objective, but to be co-creators with

> "*O Jesus,*
> MY LOVE…
> AT LAST I HAVE
> FOUND MY
> VOCATION;
> MY VOCATION
> *is Love!*"

the Lord God. He gave us the ability to grow and sustain human life, both spiritually and physically.

To understand this more deeply, we can look to St. Thérèse of Lisieux and her Little Way. In her autobiography, *The Story of a Soul*, she wrote, "Jesus, my Love, I have at last found my vocation; it is love!"[4] As women, we are called first and foremost to infuse our families, friends, and communities with love. When we tend to our own hearts and learn to recognize ourselves as divine creations, we can freely live our lives as a testimony to God's love and mercy. We can communicate who we are in Christ through our demeanor, our way of speaking, how we treat ourselves and others, and yes, how we dress.

More often than not, we reduce women to their physical appearance, ignoring their talents and strengths. The goal is to be "pretty" and "fun," without a moral compass, according to every chick flick from *She's All That* and *Mean Girls* to *The Princess Diaries* and *How to Lose a Guy in 10 Days*. There is so much more beauty to life, and *Worthy of Wearing* is a rallying cry for women who haven't found their "crowd." I want you to know that the simple fact that God created you makes you worthy, and therefore worthy of [fill in the blank]. Here's an easy equation to remember: you are made in God's image; therefore, you have dignity.

With our God-given dignity comes a sacred responsibility to be temples of the Holy Spirit. We were set apart from the rest of God's creatures because we were given the task of caring for creation, including ourselves, with intellect and reason.

Since we as Catholic Christians believe that we are a union of body and soul, we must put forth the effort to care for ourselves both inside and out. Rather than indulging in a luxurious self-care routine and avoiding the confessional,

WE WERE SET APART

from the rest of God's creatures
because we were given the task of
caring for creation, including ourselves,
with intellect and reason.

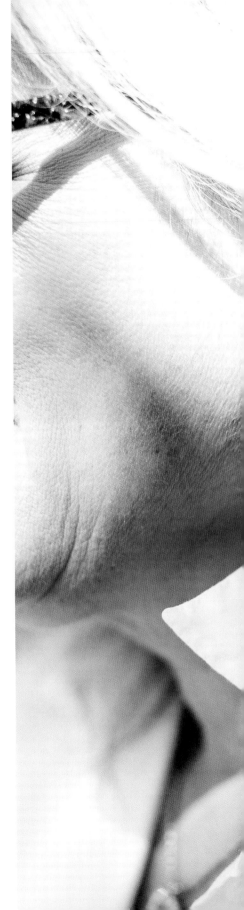

or falling into spiritual scrupulosity and neglecting personal hygiene, the modern Catholic woman finds harmony in prioritizing the care of her whole person—body and soul. Just as we must be good stewards of our bodies, so we must devote our souls to God, rooting ourselves in love. Worthy of Wearing is the attitude of adorning ourselves in a way that reveals our dignity and, in turn, makes us realize how deeply God loves us. When we are armed with that truth, and an outfit that we love, we can really do anything, come what may!

"OUR *CONCEPTION* OF CHRIST COLORS OUR WHOLE LIFE; IT INFORMS EVERYTHING WE TOUCH WITH ITS *SPIRIT*; IT MAKES US WHAT WE ARE."

— *CARYLL HOUSELANDER*
REED OF GOD

So next time you head to the bathroom in the morning, look at your reflection and see God's handiwork. Every eyelash, wrinkle, and freckle is part of His design. Use the prompts below to help you see yourself as God sees you, so you can treat yourself the way God treats you. Pray: "Lord, help me see myself the way You see me." He will.

In order to celebrate who we are, and who God created us to be, we must recognize where we are in life, because every season brings new challenges and joys. Set aside about thirty minutes to an hour to journal about these questions. They may take some time to mull over, but they are the cornerstone of uncovering who you are and, therefore, your personal style.

01. To the best of your knowledge, what is Christ calling you to right now?

02. What are some of the talents Christ has given you — as in, what comes naturally and makes you feel fulfilled when you share it with others?

03. In your current state of life, how can you use your gifts to draw more souls to Christ?

04. Which vocation do you believe Christ is calling you to?

05. What steps do you need to take to grow closer to Christ this month?

06. How do you nurture the people Christ has entrusted to you (family, friends, co-workers, members of your ministry)?

07. Whom has Christ put on your heart to reach out to or pray for?

08. How can you care for yourself this week, so that you can love others well?

CHAPTER III

CULTIVATE YOUR SELF-WORTH

Cultivate *your*

*self-*worth

What does it mean to cultivate your self-worth? Isn't it evergreen, within you from the moment of your conception? Yes, without a doubt!

But let's imagine what happens when an evergreen tree is neglected. Its branches and pine needles become hidden under choking vines, weeds, dead leaves, and spiderwebs. One might think it's just another ordinary spruce, but a more careful look reveals that it's a ponderosa pine. It has distinctive patterns on its bark, different types of pine needles and pine cones, and a story all its own.

In the same way, after many years of neglecting our self-worth, we become covered with figurative vines, weeds, and webs, usually in the form of shame, trauma, bad habits, and fear. Today — right now, in fact — we are going to change that.

Cultivating self-worth takes what may feel like backbreaking work in the form of reflection, pruning, surrender to Our Lord, and hope in the face of the Cross. Let me assure you, it is the most important work you will do in your life. Once you know your worth in Christ and lean on Him, you are free — free to live out your mission with pure intentions, a virtuous heart, and generous love of neighbor. When you begin to see how worthy you are, you will perceive, with a new clarity, the worth of every human person.

"Hearken,

O daughter, and see, and incline thine ear; for the King hath greatly desired thy beauty. With thy comeliness and thy beauty, set out, proceed prosperously, and reign."

PSALM 44: 11, 12, 5

(QUOTED IN THE 1962 ROMAN MISSAL FOR ST. CECILIA'S FEAST DAY)

Imagine Christ calling you "daughter," smiling at you in all of His glory, and saying He desires your beauty for Himself. Meditate on this scene. Put yourself in front of His heavenly throne. Know that Christ wants to use your beauty, which He instilled in you, to make your life prosper.

This verse uses two words to describe the daughter of the King. The word "comeliness" indicates her exterior appearance, while "beauty" refers to her whole being. The use of both words, when one may have sufficed, makes clear how each facet of who we are can be used for the King's glory. Christ desires our physical and spiritual beauty. He asks us to proclaim Him to the world through the beauty of our souls. He wants us to reign with Him as royalty. If we imagine the Kingdom of Heaven as a monarchy, Christ the King deems His daughters duchesses, princesses, baronesses, and countesses. He showers us with graces and talents and stands beside us in every trial we face. He fights for our protection, safety, and dreams. In fact, He places desires in our hearts so that we can realize them through our gifts and the virtues of perseverance and prudence. In this way, we bless others. At the same time, we will experience fear and doubt, not to mention mistakes, disappointments, and a few cathartic tears.

MY DAUGHTER, CECILIA

BABY NICOLE   /1990

I am no stranger to the feelings of doubt, shame, and fear that prevent me from sharing who I am with joy and vulnerability. But I didn't always feel that way. As children, we are often our truest selves — unfiltered, unbridled, and innocent. We dream our biggest dreams, dance when we want, cry without warning, and love without conditions. When presented with a blank lined page from my elementary school teacher titled "When I Grow Up...", I filled it with a list, instead of a paragraph on a single dream. At the very top was "mother," followed by "fashion designer," "writer," "dancer," "chef," and "singer in a rock band" (that last one is still to be realized). Clearly, I believed my parents' words, "You can do anything you set your mind to," which were empowering and daunting at the same time.

How could I have known exactly what God was calling me to do as an adult when I was still a child, with little life experience? Because my natural talents were encouraged, by both my teachers and my family. When I was a toddler, my dad gave me a disposable camera, and he kept the developed photos in a tiny album to show me my eye for composition. My mom let me cook dinner for the family, even when my idea of cream sauce over pasta consisted of a heaping cup of mayonnaise and a quart of sour cream. My teachers always wrote encouraging words in the margins of my book reports and essays, saying I had a gift for the written word.

MAMA & ME

My parents also gave me freedom to choose my own clothes from a young age, within the limits of what they purchased and coordinated before it entered my closet. They even tolerated my running through dance routines in every corner of the kitchen at the least convenient times of day, such as when dinner was being made. I'm not saying I grew up without rules — quite the opposite — but I had space to dream. My dad loved (and still loves) to say "Go big or go home." Little milestones, such as dance recitals and report cards, were celebrated abundantly, and I got addicted to the feeling of being good at something. It pleased others, and it made me feel as if I mattered.

FILE /UNDER   LITTLE NICOLE'S STYLE

KEY /TAKEAWAY   NECKLACES & LIPSTICK

During my early school years, I was a rule-following, book-reading good girl at school, and at home I was often singing, dancing, emoting, and telling stories, sometimes with more sass than was respectful at that age (sorry, Mom and Dad). I loved to wear dresses with Doc Martens and lace socks with overalls. And before dance class, I would unbutton a plaid flannel shirt to reveal my blush-pink leotard.

When I was in second grade, we moved to a new town. My first day at my new school, a few of the girls in my class who were sitting behind me touched my waist-length hair, which my mom had curled, and said, "Your hair is so pretty." I turned around, smiled, and said thank you. Another girl a few seats behind me snorted to her friends, "The new girl is so stuck up." My face went hot, and suddenly I felt knots in my stomach. The teacher's words became muted in my mind, and I wanted to go home. All at once, the idea of being a princess, the daughter of a King, was a cause for pain. It was then that I decided I wanted to blend in.

I was a good girl at school, but desired a community I could rest in. At home, I was boisterous and snarky at times, but wanted to be heard and respected. The two competing sides of my temperament—one extroverted side that needed an audience to make life more fun, and one studious and phlegmatic side that processed and analyzed everything—made it difficult to feel as though I truly belonged. Hiding my interior difficulties seemed like the best choice at the time, but looking back, I wish I had reached out more. Instead, I developed a bad habit of shifting facades depending on my environment, without yet knowing the moral implications of living a double life.

In fifth grade, the delicately balanced two sides were forced apart as if by a tectonic plate shift. The chasm in the middle was widened by the all-consuming struggles of insecurity, being bullied, and feeling as though no one understood me. Fear of being exposed or embarrassed made it difficult to trust anyone.

circa '02

Nicole

As puberty came, I saw the shape of my body change in what felt like a single week. Suddenly, my hair was greasy every afternoon, my skin broke out with painful acne, and my pharmacy shopping list included razors and those things you really don't want to ask your dad to buy for your monthly cycle. My stomach puffed out and often felt squished under the button of my jeans. Soon, I had to start shopping in the women's section of Gap because the glitter-strewn T-shirts and shorts in the kids' section no longer fit my developing figure.

My first selfie!

The next layer in the confusion of my identity came when I had to choose what kind of woman I wanted to be, since I now had a woman's body. I envied the girlish clothes my peers wore. My classmates were years behind me hormonally, and being around them for eight hours a day made me loathe the new phase of life I had entered. Recess was my least favorite time of the school day. My female peers often gathered in small circles, giggling at the girls like me who didn't have a clique. The guys just wanted to play sports, but I was so uncoordinated and lost in my own thoughts that they wouldn't let me play. I was stuck in limbo.

One day, when I was feeling particularly crampy and uncomfortable with my premature experience of womanhood, a classmate noticed a stain on the back of my pants. She naïvely thought I had just sat in something. My face turned hotter than a griddle. I knew what the real problem was. And there was no way to hide it, no matter how much I spun the roll of toilet paper in the girls' bathroom and dabbed and dabbed. At recess, I tried to blend in with the teachers supervising, but I couldn't escape the looks, pointing fingers, and snickers coming from the circles of girls a few yards away.

Being at school was painful, and my friend group went from three members to one (luckily for me, my British expat neighbor didn't abandon our friendship). To survive the moments I couldn't be with my one and only friend, I did what I could: I tried to be like the other girls. Magazines such as *Teen People, Seventeen,* and *Lucky* became my insider's guide to what these "other girls" were like. I read and researched, and I locked

GENERATIONS OF *WOMEN* IN MY FAMILY

MY BEAUTIFUL MOTHER
& MY DAUGHTER

away away every dream in my heart to make myself more palatable to my classmates. I fell into the lie that to be strong, I had to hide my sensitive heart. People-pleasing was my game, and I lost sight of my identity in the process. Only after becoming a mother did I learn that a sensitive heart is an immense gift.

I chopped off my long hair to a chin-length bob, started "preferring" sweater sets and pearls (even though I was a jean-jacket-and-gemstone kind of girl), and begged my parents for a navy L. L. Bean backpack with my initials for every gift-giving holiday until it was finally mine. I also begged them for New Balance sneakers, a North Face fleece jacket, and a Kate Spade pencil case — status symbols in Fairfield County, Connecticut, in the late 1990s and early 2000s. But we weren't a high-status family. Shortly after I moved to my new school, my dad lost his job and started his own landscaping business. It was backbreaking work, and he often came home so drenched in sweat that his leather belt was damp to the touch. Before long, my classmates saw my dad cutting their lawns and weeding their gardens, and they bullied me, despite my best efforts to become invisible. Once again, the cool kids wanted to show me that I'd never matter to them, even if I had a navy blue L. L. Bean backpack.

The importance of popularity, financial status, academic and athletic performance, and perfection was drilled into our twelve-year-old minds. The messaging from popular culture that celebrated crude humor, objectification, promiscuity, materialism, and workaholism started during those years and, sadly, infiltrated pure little hearts like mine. I know I'm not the only one who suffered the daily battles of teasing, dealing with bossy friends and apathetic teachers, and trying to fit in. The voices that cut me down remained in my mind and had a strong hold over how I thought of myself. I didn't realize how much they affected me daily until well after I had entered the workforce. I could give many examples of harsh words that were said to me, or behind my back, but they will not aid your journey, just as they did not aid mine. All I know is that when I felt unlovable and undesirable, destroying my self-worth was a slippery slope. On top of that, the media I consumed portrayed girls like me as goody two-shoes, prudes, and teacher's pets. Is that what our culture thinks of women who aim to follow the Ten Commandments, respect their bodies, and strive for excellence? You know the answer.

AN ALL-AMERICAN LOOK
FOR CECILIA AND HER GIGI

Comparison bullies us into constantly observing others and losing touch with who we are. Rather than celebrating our unique and unrepeatable nature, we fall into the lie that one woman's beauty or success means our ugliness or failure. It is natural to see and admire the beauty of others, but admiration can quickly turn to comparison when we remove Christ from the center of our lives. Envy, jealousy, and even self-hatred will slowly seep into our thoughts if we are not rooted in self-awareness. God purposefully designed our lives for the exact moment in which we exist. Our strengths, weaknesses, talents, temperaments, vocations, and circumstances are the path to wholeness. All of us face adversity. All of us endure suffering and trials. What we do with these obstacles develops our character and gives us opportunities to love more deeply and to rely on Christ to carry us through every single day. Rooted in His love, we can celebrate who we are, knowing our purpose is to share His truth, beauty, and goodness with the people He places in our lives.

When we lose our identity, our lifestyle choices and personal style are the first to go with it. Have you ever doubted that you were seen and loved by your community and family, or by God? Have you thought your life didn't matter, or have you lost yourself while trying to "find yourself"? In our culture, where truth is subjective and human life is valued only when convenient, the smoke of confusion surrounds us. We are told to empower ourselves while marginalizing others. We are told "good girls rarely make history" — an empty catchphrase that female saints such as St. Gianna Molla, St. Teresa Benedicta of the Cross, St. Teresa of Calcutta, and hundreds of others have been disproving for centuries.

The difficulties I experienced at school, combined with an anemic faith life until my reversion in high school, set the stage for my struggle with confidence and self-worth. I began battling impostor syndrome even before I knew what it was. In pursuit of a social life, I blocked out the strong voice of my conscience, gave up on my faith, ignored my family, and made many other foolish decisions. Those choices led to more painful experiences than I could have imagined. I lost touch with my purpose, and I almost lost my soul. My desire to be desired was obvious from how I engaged in people-pleasing, bent the rules, and buried my true values.

Once college came, I wanted to be different. I was tired of being "me" and wanted to freshen things up, or so I thought. Craving more control over how others judged me, I thought it best to craft my image myself. From all the magazines I read, I knew "success" looked like dominating my peer group and having a girl gang who loved but mostly feared you, à la *Mean Girls*. I chose to wear the clothes my friends wore. I shopped at the same stores, and even though I felt so "different," we looked like little clones whenever we went out in a group. No matter how much I tried to be this "new" me, the heaviness of my inauthenticity was weighing on me. It was a lot of work to be someone else, as my new group of drama-frenzied friends and my first-quarter grades demonstrated. My identity crisis showed up in my clothing, my friend group, my skewed morality, and various coping mechanisms, such as dressing for attention, obsessing over boy crushes, lashing out at my family, and drowning out my pain with loud music, celebrity gossip, and reality TV.

God gave me the grace to crash and burn — truly — before things could get much worse. His mercy abounds. A manipulative dating relationship made me hit rock bottom. That shake-up turned me around and allowed me to heal from the inside out. When you hit rock bottom, you can either linger there or try to get out of it as fast as you got there. My parents, my close friends, a Catholic psychologist, dear priest-friends of my family, the mother of one of my best friends, and my spiritual director from high school enveloped me with support. I transferred out of that university, got rid of everything that reminded me of my time there, and started over. God blessed me with a substitute-teaching job at our local Catholic school. Being around innocent children reminded me of who I was. Their jokes, smiles, and stories delighted me. I enrolled in a state university to finish my degree and, with the protection of being unknown on campus, began to rebuild my self-worth.

NUN CCO EPI

MEANING: *Now I begin.* ORIGIN: *From the Vulgate, the Latin translation of the Bible*

I poured my heart into my studies, my therapy sessions, and my faith. I embraced the beautiful Latin phrase made popular by St. Josemaría Escrivá: "Nunc coepi," meaning "Now I begin."

We all have that chance, right now and every day, to begin again. Know that truth, and let it enter your heart. Like Mary Magdalene, you can be created anew in Christ, no matter your past struggles or current battles. I've learned now to pay attention to the women in Scripture to whom Christ paid attention. The way He loved those women teaches us so much about His love.

Rather than fitting ourselves to our culture's idea of womanhood, we can simply embrace who God created us to be, then share His light with the world. Reigning with God, as Pope John Paul II explains in his *Letter to Women*, means revealing the *imago Dei* — the image of God — that we bear. We were made to be attracted to beauty, as God created it to point to Himself. Beauty stirs the soul, gives rise to wonder, catches us in an ordinary moment and reveals something extraordinary. But beauty for its own sake, without Christ as its end, is beauty in vain. "In vain" is one of those phrases we hear in faith circles. Simply put, it refers to any action that is not Christ-centered or that prioritizes our own pleasure over the teachings of Christ.

Remember, a flame cannot burn when it is cut off from air. Exposing who we are in Christ, though it may be hard at first, gives our flame oxygen so it can burn and bring forth His light. Make an Act of Faith and say, "Jesus, I trust in You." He desires our wholeness, and will provide every grace necessary to sustain us.

01. Write about a moment that damaged your confidence. How did that experience change the way you saw the world, Christ, and the Father?

02. Name three fears that hold you back from letting Christ love you as you are.

03. Name three insecurities that prevent you from going after your dreams.

04. List three things you dream of doing before you die.

05. What would you do today if you had no fear?

06. List your top five talents and spiritual gifts. Not sure what they are? The resources section can help you get started. In particular, you might look at the book *StrengthsFinder 2.0* and its accompanying assessment, as well as the Catherine of Siena Institute's Called & Gifted Study, to discover your spiritual gifts.

07. To the best of your knowledge, what is your life's mission?

08. How do you feel God is calling you to live your mission in the present moment?

UNCOVER YOUR FEARS AND BE SET FREE

Set aside thirty minutes to an hour to reflect on and journal about the prompts on this page.

CHAPTER IV

OWN
YOUR
STORY

Own your

your

Story

including the ones I imagine while people-watching. When I was a kid, my dad would call me "Nosy Nikki" because no matter where we went, I just wanted to observe people. I loved seeing the changes in their faces when they spoke, the hand gestures they made, their clothing and mannerisms, and the stories they told. From a young age, I walked around with a two-by-three-inch lined notebook in which to record my thoughts and observations. From this data, I would create a story about the people I saw. It was great fun, and the material became the subject of many short stories I scribbled into notebooks or wrote for fiction essays at school. If I didn't love sharing style and beauty with women so much, I think I would have made a great novelist.

Each of us has a story. The moment of our birth was a mystery planned beyond our understanding. Our story is an integral part of who we are and what we're made for. Every experience leading up to this moment, as you are holding this book in your hands, is part of your story. Even painful experiences are an important part of the narrative of your life, since our response to these experiences informs our character and helps us grow in virtue. Take personal development guru Tony Robbins, for example. He had an abusive and traumatic childhood, but he didn't let that difficult experience prevent him from greatness. What could have led to a life of numbing his pain instead fueled his success. A self-made millionaire, he now spends his time sharing his financial, business, and personal practices to help others reach their potential. As he explains, "If my mom had been the mother I thought I wanted, I wouldn't be as driven; I wouldn't be as hungry ... I wouldn't have suffered, so I probably wouldn't have cared about other people's suffering as much as I do. And it made me obsessed with wanting to understand people and help create change."[5]

Do we let our trials define us, or do we use them to grow? And, when we realize our mistakes, do we own up to them? Think of the story of George Washington and the cherry

> "
>
> *IF MY MOM HAD BEEN THE MOTHER I THOUGHT I WANTED, I WOULDN'T BE AS DRIVEN; I WOULDN'T BE AS HUNGRY.*
>
> (HE SAID)
>
> *I WOULDN'T HAVE SUFFERED, SO I PROBABLY WOULDN'T HAVE CARED ABOUT OTHER PEOPLE'S SUFFERING AS MUCH AS I DO. AND IT MADE ME OBSESSED WITH WANTING TO UNDERSTAND PEOPLE AND HELP CREATE CHANGE.*
>
> "

tree, He took his ax to his father's beloved tree, which he then left for dead. His father found it and asked him what happened. George confessed. Legend has it, his father commended him for being brave enough to tell the truth. What a meaningful story! I like to think our Father in Heaven is twice as merciful when we come to Him after falling into sin.

WE MAY

WANT TO BE THE KIND OF WOMAN WHO WAKES UP EARLY TO KICKSTART HER DAY, BUT ALL TOO OFTEN, WE NEVER ACTUALLY TAKE THE STEPS OF SETTING OUR ALARM TO 5:00 A.M. AND GOING TO BED EARLY THE NIGHT BEFORE. SINCE YOU'RE READING THIS BOOK, YOU PROBABLY WANT TO BE A WOMAN OF INTEGRITY, A WOMAN OF FAITH, AND A STYLISH WOMAN, SO WHAT CONCRETE STEPS CAN YOU TAKE TO GET THERE?

THE FIRST IS TO DEVELOP YOUR SELF-AWARENESS.

All of us are faced with choices on a daily basis that can drive us closer to God or away from Him. We can respond with virtue, or we can stay in our comfort zone. Either way, we must choose. Life in Christ is not static. Even lukewarmness causes us to move away from Him, because we are always in motion, like the earth, moving either closer to or further away from our center — the Son.

Responding with heroic virtue often means doing the right thing when it's the most painful— for example, hopping out of bed the second the alarm goes off, instead of snoozing a dozen times. It's all too easy to choose to stay comfortable. We may want to be the kind of woman who wakes up early to kick-start her day, but all too often, we never actually take the steps of setting our alarm to 5:00 a.m. and going to bed early the night before. Since you're reading this book, you probably want to be a woman of integrity, a woman of faith, and a *stylish* woman, so what concrete steps can you take to get there? The first is to develop your self-awareness.

The familiar phrase "wear your heart on your sleeve" can be traced back to Shakespeare's *Othello* (act 1, scene 1, lines 56–65). Our hearts are chambers of life, sustaining our existence and holding our past. Just as the Eucharist in the tabernacle is covered with a jacquard veil, some parts of our hearts are kept hidden because they are too precious to reveal openly. Other parts we share so the people in our lives can know and return our love.

Wearing one style of clothing on our sleeves with something entirely different in our heart creates dissonance. We don't always consciously choose to misrepresent ourselves; sometimes, we simply lack confidence. To be more confident in ourselves, to create the internal harmony that we express outwardly with our personal style, we have to accept our story, the good with the bad, and use it to bring solace and inspiration to others. We do this by recognizing who we are, acknowledging our talents, and believing that Christ is guiding us.

Personal style is like the cover of a book. A single image or string of type cannot tell all; rather, it offers a glimpse of what the book is about. A frilly, ultra-femme style gives off childlike whimsy; punk style is synonymous with rebellion and grit; bohemian hippie style is often equated with a laissez-faire outlook; sporty style indicates focused athletic drive; and schoolgirl preppy style lends itself to a prim and proper vibe. Our clothing tells a story, but which story do we want it to tell? How would you design the cover of the book about your life?

One of the first times I remember seeing a Star of David was on an elementary school classmate's necklace. Made of polished sterling

Q

ONE

Which story do we want it to tell?

TWO

How would you design the cover of the book about your life?

silver and scant the size of my pinky nail, it caught the light when she brushed her long curls over her shoulder. I asked her what it was, and she explained her love for her Jewish faith. We had never spoken before, but that little shining star was the starting point from which a relationship could begin.

What is something you wear that tells a little part of your story? Every single day, I wear my diamond wedding band, which is both understated and a little fancy; a St. Benedict Medal; a Miraculous Medal; and a necklace with my kids' initials. With one glance, you can see my heart: my devotion to my Catholic Faith, how dear my husband is to me, and how blessed I feel to be a mother.

Everything, down to our choice of shoes, speaks without words. Southwestern Connecticut, where I grew up, is known for its classic, preppy, and even equestrian-chic style.

r

Your
FAMILY HISTORY,
BELIEFS,
LOCALITY,
HOBBIES,
TRAVEL
EXPERIENCES,
HEARTACHES,
JOYS, & DREAMS —
ALL THESE
INSPIRE YOUR
personal style.

A piece of Connecticut's understated luxury will always be part of my story, and for that reason, I often wear pared-down basics all year round, such as a white collared shirt, simple blue jeans, and a double-breasted blazer.

What part of the world has influenced your style story? Maybe you grew up near the beach, so you are attracted to items with a seaside feel, such as leather sandals, crocheted textures, pops of bright color, and large prints. Or maybe your family had a weekend hiking route, so you love an outdoorsy flair of rubber-soled boots and layered tops. Even if you live in the Midwest, but liked the Parisian fashions you saw on your study-abroad trip last summer, your style might have a heavy Parisian influence of high-end and low-end labels. Likewise, if you spent your whole life in the Pacific Northwest, well known as the birthplace of the grunge era, but your recent move to a cozy neighborhood outside of New Orleans has made you fully embrace the vibrant Cajun atmosphere, you may replace your favorite buffalo-check plaid with an unexpected splash of color. Your family history, beliefs, locality, hobbies, travel experiences, heartaches, joys, and dreams — all these inspire your personal style.

We can dress ourselves to communicate anything we like, but we do a big disservice to who we are when those pieces tell a story that is not our own. You can shop the most fashionable outfit right off the runway and not look stylish if it doesn't express who you are. When I wanted to fit in with my peers in college, I tried wearing clothes that were a little shorter, tighter, and trendier. This attracted unwanted attention from guys who weren't looking at me as a potential friend, but as a potential fling. After a few experiences of feeling shockingly objectified, I went back to my roots of jeans and collared shirts. It just felt more me, and my potential suitors seemed to evaporate into thin air. I still incorporated the trends I loved, but I felt more authentic experimenting with accessories, makeup, and hairstyles, rather than my daily uniform. Almost overnight, the pivot made a world of difference.

My clothing comfort zone turned out to be a baseline that I desperately needed to return to, for my own self-worth and in order to project my real story.

I want you to be empowered by just how worthy you are. You're worthy of changing your personal style to better suit the life you are living and the mission you are pursuing right now. Maybe you used to love a certain style years ago, but it just doesn't work for the season of life you're currently in (more on this in chapter 9). Style evolves because the human person does. As we grow and change, our style grows and changes — as it should. Every year, I make little tweaks to hone my style, and as a result, I feel more and more myself when I get dressed. Personal style is a compilation of who we are, where we've been, and where we want to go in life.

Now, I'd like to share a little more about my story and give you a peek into how my personal style came to be. I took my first breath in Mount Sinai Hospital on the Upper West Side of Manhattan. I'm a New Yorker at heart. Though we lived an hour outside the city, I always felt less connected to my Connecticut peers than to the complete strangers I saw while walking in Midtown or Nolita. Every time I returned, I felt I was exactly where I was supposed to be. My whole soul was swept up in the lights, sounds, stunning architecture, and bustle of the city. Brisk autumn nights were my favorite times to marvel at the amber-lit windows of the homes of mysterious city people with stories I desperately wanted to know. One time on 42nd Street, I caught a glimpse of a city mom pushing her baby in a sleek stroller while her ponytail whipped behind her. She was wearing a black knee-length anorak, black shiny leggings, black cross-trainer sneakers, and big round black sunglasses. I gasped. Her style was so magnetic. "That's gonna be me," I decided immediately. We can call her my first style icon — after my mama, of course.

Fashion was our family business, so it's been a part of my story since even before I was born. My parents locked eyes at a garment industry trade show for womenswear in 1983, and five autumns later, I was born. My

FILE /UNDER   PERSONAL BACKSTORY

SUBJECT /THEME   SENSE OF STYLE

family has its roots in fashion and the city that never sleeps not only because my parents worked in the fashion industry but also because they love personal style — my dad even more so than my mom. My earliest style memories include white lace-trimmed socks on Easter, a cheetah-print swimsuit for summer days by the pool, velvet dresses at Christmas, and many pairs of Oshkosh B'gosh overalls in between. I connected clothing with milestones and memories: a red beret when I saw the Rockettes at Christmas, a baggy lake-blue windbreaker for the first day of my last year of elementary school, and a turquoise top embroidered with Funfetti-style beads for a spring choir concert. A silver Fossil watch with a blue-green metal face marked my tenth birthday. Clothing was not only my way of collecting memories; it was also a language for communicating my moods, my inspirations, and my stage of life.

During family trips to the Sagamore Resort in Lake George, New York, I realized for the first time that the way I behaved and dressed told other people something about me, about how I wanted to be seen and treated. As strangers passed us in the dining room, they would exclaim, "What beautiful girls!" My sister and I would look up with our baby-teeth smiles and cheerily say thank you in unison, just as our parents had taught

Hello Gorgeous

us. Adults were always in awe of our matching outfits and good manners, and truthfully, the waitstaff and other guests treated us like little princesses because we acted as such. (I imagine this partly explains why the British royal family has long upheld traditional customs and dress codes. The consistency itself also commands respect.) We did not dress "to impress," as in vainly dressing for the attention of others, but we did create a story with our body language and what we wore.

At the other extreme, women have shared stories with me of being catcalled while walking city streets in a bodycon dress and heeled boots. Others have told me about feeling violated by the wandering looks they get when wearing a V-neck or a fitted shirt. I've had my fair share of these experiences, and they haven't been tied to any consistent outfit "type"; however, it's true that the lines and shapes of our clothes can direct an onlooker's eyes. Our gaze is naturally attracted to angles, such as the tip of a V-neck, just as an eye follows an arrow. A crop top has a line that cuts across the ribcage, so the eye is drawn to the end of the garment. If the only thing underneath is skin, that's what people will look at. In other words, items such as cut-outs, crop tops, and second-skin fabrics draw attention to one part of the outfit as opposed to the whole look. My experience has shown that when I clothe myself in a way that is authentic to who I am — highlighting not one body part but my whole person — the people I meet greet me respectfully, with eye contact. It's important to be more intentional about how our clothes fit and move with us throughout the day. (Read more in chapter 7 about how to take your clothes for a test drive.)

Your story matters, and what you wear matters. Regardless of how interested you are in fashion, you do have a style. Your style could be youth-group tees and jeans because that's what you have the most of, and it is a style. What do you want your style to say about you? Each day, when you get dressed, be bold about who you are. It's so important to have childlike confidence, as those Thanksgivings and Easters at Lake George showed me. Accepting a compliment, an acknowledgment that you are seen and loved, can be a step toward recognizing your worth.

The biggest step toward feeling worthy is inviting Christ into your story. Write down the moments of your life when He showed Himself to you. Sometimes a complete stranger can speak God's truth right to our heart without knowing anything about us. Ask Jesus to heal your hurts, thank Him for your blessings, and invite Him into your present. He desperately wants to love you, to guide you, and to use your gifts to lead others to Him.

If you're still feeling as though uncovering your personal style will take some time, that is completely normal! This is not an overnight process. Be patient with yourself, and "be brave in the scared," as my friend Mary Lenaburg encourages in her book of the same title. And remember, the Holy Spirit happens to be really great at finding the perfect item you've been dreaming of wearing, at the perfect price — just ask me how I know. Trust in Him.

01. How did your story begin? Where were you born, where did you live, what was your family like, and what was your understanding of God?

02. What is your fondest memory from childhood? What about your fondest memory from recent times? How did these moments affect you? Who was by your side?

03. What is your most difficult memory from childhood? What is a difficulty you currently face? How did you get through these difficulties? Who was by your side?

04. How do your personality, family, and life experiences influence what you wear?

05. What does your clothing communicate about who you are and who you aspire to be?

06. What do you want others to know about you from your clothing?

07. Which items in your closet misrepresent who you are? (Get rid of them!)

08. Which item in your closet do you treasure the most?

09. What outfit do you wear to feel confident? (Wear it more!)

10. What would you accomplish if you had no limitations? What would you wear while pursuing these dreams?

OWN YOUR STORY

Light a candle, curl up, and give yourself some time to reflect on what you can recall from your life, from your first memories to the present moment.

two

IN A
CATHOLIC
CONTEXT

THE INTEGRATED, MODERN CATHOLIC WOMAN

modern

CATHOLIC

woman

What does it mean

to be integrated and modern when our hearts are set on Heaven? As Catholic women, we desire to be holy and to spend the rest of eternity with Our Lord. We understand the beauty of deep prayer, intimacy with Christ, and the examples of saints such as St. Francis of Assisi and St. Anthony of the Desert, who gave away all their possessions to follow God.

Still, our daily reality may seem to pull us in the opposite direction. Distractions from the pursuit of a faith life abound in the form of technology overuse, concern over social expectations, earning a living, politics, and the lure of loosening our moral standards. Adopting the ways of this world is easy because life here is tangible. All too quickly, however, we can become preoccupied with worldly success, popularity, and material wealth. In doing so, we lose sight of the purpose God ordained for our lives.

So should we imitate the solitary ascetics of past centuries in rejecting popular culture and dedicating ourselves to a life of prayer? Or should we commit ourselves to making the most of this life, reserving matters of faith for old age? The short answer is neither. Our duty is to live in the world without being of the world.

One of my favorite phrases to reflect on is "MEMENTO MORI," meaning "Remember that you must die." Our world is God's creation. We can delight in it, but it is not our forever home, just a pathway to the eternal. Living life while being mindful of our mortality puts everything into perspective. We waste less time, grow in zeal, and let go of prideful inhibitions that prevent us from accomplishing God's plan.

If you knew you had only a month to live, would you live differently?

Jesus called out to the first apostles with a simple, complete sentence: "Follow Me." He invited them, in the midst of their ordinary lives, to be extraordinary ambassadors for His Kingdom under His loving guidance. Likewise, He has called each of us to follow Him in our daily lives and to serve in different ways: as dedicated singles, members of a religious order, wives, spiritual or biological mothers, widows, daughters, sisters, and friends.

Here on earth, we do our best to live for Christ, but we also have to assimilate our surroundings and continue to be relevant to our peers. St. Paul wrote: "To the weak I became weak, to win over the weak. I have

"

THE
WORLD
IS THY
SHIP,
AND NOT
THY
HOME.

"

ST. THÉRÈSE
OF LISIEUX

become all things to all, to save at least some" (1 Cor. 9:22). His message encourages us to be relevant to others in the world, while maintaining our Christian worldview. This, St. Paul explains, is the secret to touching many lives. The way we live will teach souls what being a Christian is all about.

Once, a speaker at a retreat said something that I still ponder to this day: "If a video camera was following you around all day, would the viewer know you are a Catholic?" These words made me realize how much I resisted appearing "religious." At that time, I didn't even want to cross myself before eating a meal in a café.

If we want to preach the Gospel in our workplace, we have to be diligent and professional as we labor alongside our co-workers. If we want to preach the Gospel in our college classroom, we have to be relevant enough to our peers that they pay attention when we speak. If we want our daughters and nieces to learn how to rise in the world without falling for its lies, we have to teach them through our example. All of this requires being faithful in the little things and striving for virtue.

Our role as Catholic Christian women is to save souls by representing Christ in our calling and making our devout life look attractive. I am Catholic, *and* I love style, art, history, travel, music, business, and design. My faith is the reason for everything I do, *and* God placed certain interests on my heart when He created me. He has shown me over the years not to listen to the sneering voices that try to pull me toward one extreme or the other, but to listen to Him. He determines the balance point and guides me toward it.

When you embrace certain aspects of modernity (within the bounds of Catholic teaching), you make the Gospel attractive. You demonstrate that anyone can turn his or her life over to Christ and still make a difference in the world, without being as radical as St. Francis of Assisi and abandoning every earthly possession.

As many of you have told me, however, it's not easy to balance being relevant and upholding your faith, and don't I know it. On the one hand, religious women have been fed the lie that we should not waste time on our appearance because style is vain, frivolous, self-centered, and worldly. Sadly, many of the faithful have helped spread this lie. They think high heels, bejeweled earrings, and lipstick erase virtue and the desire for holiness. This attitude is so prevalent that at faith-based events, I always used to feel the need to tone down my outfits, blend in more, and steer clear of overdressing. On the other hand, many people in the secular world struggle to understand why our faith is the center of our lives. When I worked in fashion, my personal style was celebrated, but one flash of my wedding ring was all it took to puzzle my co-workers. They'd ask: "How old are you? When did you get married?" My choice to marry young made them think I was an extremist. And sadly, they didn't understand the beauty of the Sacrament of Marriage.

Most of us lack a bridge between our faith life and our life in the working world. With this book, I want to help you start building that bridge. Faith culture and secular culture try not to overlap, but I have learned that grace can be found when the two meet. When we integrate the two, we stop living a double life and begin to live one wholly fulfilling life.

WORTHY OF WEARING

When I was in high school, some young professional women in Manhattan invited me to their weekly Gospel reflection group at the Lumen Center in the Lincoln Building (now known as One Grand Central Place), across from Grand Central Station.

Walking into the conference room with my Chuck Taylor sneakers and flared jeans, I was immediately struck by the beauty of the women in the group. They had arrived from their corporate jobs all over the city with their nails painted, makeup on, and hair blown out. One was wearing tones of cream and camel from head to toe, with stunning minimalist gold jewelry. All of them were simultaneously chic and ageless.

During the meeting, the women poured out their hearts, sharing inspirations and prayer intentions. Afterward, we all went out for burgers. We laughed uproariously over our plates of French fries, shared nightmarish dating stories, and walked arm in arm, still laughing, back to Grand Central to take the train home. The night was nothing short of a New York dream.

Those women taught me what it means to be in the world, but not of it. We can't be pigeonholed as either "religious" or "worldly"; instead, we have unique, multifaceted stories. When we embrace these stories and live an integrated life, we reveal Christ to the world. So let's reclaim our femininity and dignity, which emanate from the One Who believes in us.

Living an integrated life means caring for our whole selves. We are an unrepeatable union of body and soul, and we feel our best when we attend to both. Taking ten minutes in the morning to get dressed, moisturize our skin, and brush our hair can make all the difference for our mood and the way we see ourselves. Similarly, going to Holy Mass and Reconciliation lifts the heaviness of our worldly cares, gives meaning to what is ordinary, and refocuses our gaze on our ultimate goal: Heaven. When we tend to our needs before getting on with the day, we can serve the needs of others with more zeal and interior peace.

"

For it was (you)
WHO CREATED MY BEING, KNIT ME IN MY MOTHER'S WOMB.
I THANK YOU FOR THE *(wonder)* OF MY BEING,
FOR THE WONDERS OF ALL YOUR *(creation)*. ALREADY YOU KNEW
MY *(soul)*, MY BODY HELD NO SECRET FROM *(you)* WHEN
I WAS BEING FASHIONED IN SECRET AND MOLDED
in the depths of the earth."

PSALM 139 [138]:13–15
(GRAIL TRANSLATION)

The truth is, faith and fashion go together. God didn't just make beauty; He is beauty. All of creation is a reflection of His beauty. Just imagine what it would be like if we lived in a world without the majesty of nature. Would we ever stop to wonder about its Creator?

When we recognize, cultivate, and celebrate our own inherent beauty, both inside and out, we can change hearts. When we do the hard work of uniting our interior and our exterior, we can be light for a world darkened by pain and suffering, and when we take care of ourselves in a way that is authentic to who we are and is neither self-seeking nor steeped in vanity, we become unstoppable. The Holy Spirit will bless our every task. He will give us grace, protect us from harm, and empower us to do far more than we could alone.

Do you know you're beautiful? I know you are. God does too. If you struggle with recognizing your beauty, remember that the media's standard of beauty represents only a fraction of God's creation. The world overlooks and ignores the many ways a woman can be beautiful, but God does not. He knows your worth and your dignity.

"I CAN TAKE CARE OF MYSELF, AND JUST THIS LITTLE BIT OF CARE CHANGES THE WAY I FEEL.

"I HONESTLY FORGOT HOW GREAT I FEEL WHEN I TAKE THE TIME TO DRESS UP."

EVERY DAY."

HERE ARE A FEW MESSAGES YOU HAVE SHARED WITH ME ABOUT HOW THESE IDEAS HAVE RESONATED WITH YOU:

In his Apostolic Letter *Mulieris Dignitatem* (On the Dignity and Vocation of Women), Pope St. John Paul II wrote: "The dignity of every human being and the vocation corresponding to that dignity find their definitive measure *in union with God*. Mary, the woman of the Bible, is the most complete expression of this dignity and vocation. For no human being, male or female, created in the image and likeness of God, can *in any way* attain fulfillment apart from this image and likeness."[6]

Our fulfillment as women of faith and women living in the world comes from God alone. It is in the expression of our dignity and our vocation that we intertwine the eternal with the material. How we live our life, how we dress, how we serve in our mission, how we treat others — all are ways of bringing God into the world.

"O LORD,

YOU SEARCH ME AND YOU
KNOW ME, YOU KNOW MY
RESTING AND MY RISING,
YOU DISCERN MY PURPOSE
FROM AFAR."

PSALM 139 [138]:1–2
(GRAIL TRANSLATION)

CHAPTER VI

RECLAIMING STYLE FROM FASHION

reclaiming

STYLE

from

FASHION

Let's take a moment

to talk about fashion, which is often equated with style. If you've ever flipped through a magazine, scrolled through an influencer's photos, or watched an awards show, you've seen the hold that fashion has on our culture. Fashion is an industry, a business like any other. The fashion industry employs designers, sales executives, buyers, and press teams, not to mention seamstresses, tailors, hand-embroiderers, zipper whizzes, and button aficionados.

Most of what we see in fashion comes from cultural trends (think popular films, music videos, and performances), the latest designs from big brands, and the colors, silhouettes, and pairings that influencers and celebrities have popularized. These ideals often misrepresent women, although that has begun to change over the past decade, thanks to a handful of designers. Historically, the fashion industry has presented women as either waifish, victimized objects or powerful, regretless objectifiers. Never mind that I can't relate to these women, or that I wouldn't want my daughter to emulate them — year after year, the fashion industry has continued to insist that it is the authority on what's "in." Flip through any issue of *Vogue* or *InStyle* and prove me wrong.

As Dr. Carrie Gress eloquently explains in her book *The Anti-Mary Exposed:* "The fashion industry . . . sets the standard for what 'beautiful' women are supposed to look like. What they mean by beautiful is a whole lot different than what beauty is really meant to be. Here againis the chasm between our culture and Mary, between a 'beauty' of sexual objectification and a true beauty that stirs the soul, pulls us out of ourselves, and lifts the heart and mind to the Creator of all things."[7]

For a short but intense time, I worked for two different fashion houses in Manhattan's Garment District. The first was founded by a female American designer whose entrepreneurial work ethic I deeply admired, and the second was an Italian fashion house that made everything from couture to baby clothes. My goal was to learn as much as I could about how the industry worked, in the hopes of uncovering the plan God had in mind for me. It was cool, of course, mostly because I had many "pinch me" moments that fulfilled my childhood dreams, such as when I dressed models backstage for New York Fashion Week at Lincoln Center, then peeked into the dressing room next door to watch hair legend Orlando Pita style Karolína Kurková's hair. Not only did I get to see the backstage chaos that reminded me of my dance recital days, but I got to watch a few shows from inside the tents and experience the heart palpitations of live music blaring with alarmingly beautiful women adorned in incredible clothes strutting down long runways. It was unforgettable. In the end, the reality of working in fashion was mostly long hours swirled with emotional strain. It took such a toll on my body, heart, and marriage that I left the entire industry much sooner than I expected, even though I had a great opportunity on the table.

As the saying goes, when God closes a door, He opens a window. After returning to my work as a makeup artist, I became the beauty editor of *Verily* magazine. Its co-founders, Kara Eschbach and Janet Easter, didn't believe the industry's lie that women had to conform to be seen as beautiful. Many women found our tagline — "Less of who you should be, more of who you are" — refreshing. *Verily* was the first publication to feature women of all sizes as models, and the magazine pioneered the movement to ditch Photoshop. Our team wanted to show women what was missing in most media: the truth that we are beautiful and worthy because of who we are and Who made us, not because of how we dress or what we own. In other words, we don't need the fashion industry to tell us how to be stylish. We don't need tabloids, red carpets, or reality TV. Embracing what is good, true, and beautiful makes us stylish. How we wear our clothes, regardless of who designed them, determines our style.

Let's do something together, right now. Let's reclaim style from the fashion industry. Famous designers and big-name brands don't own personal style. We don't need to follow their arbitrary rules, such as not wearing white after Labor Day. (Winter white is chic!) Let's commit to cultivating our style, no matter what the fashion industry might think of it.

To understand what makes style different from fashion, imagine a bride on her wedding day. Is her dress white or ecru? Is it lace or satin? Maybe it's beaded. Does it have a train, or is it tea length? Did the bride have her mother sew a Miraculous Medal into the dress? Is she wearing a pair of blue heels under the tulle? Her hair could be curled, straight, up, or down. Maybe she's wearing her grandmother's veil or her sister's bracelet. Her lipstick might be rose-colored or red.

That's what style is: the way you adorn yourself within various contexts to express who you are uniquely, boldly, and unapologetically. It is a method of getting dressed, presenting your appearance, and telling your story without speaking. Style means intentionally choosing clothing that speaks to your mission, fuels your confidence, and creates connections with others by offering a little peek of who you are. In this way, style is more edifying than fashion.

We can put our own spin on any article of clothing. My sister and I often buy the same clothes. We both own black jeans, striped shirts, and white sundresses, but we wear them differently. Paired with a circle skirt, hoop earrings, and leather sandals, a striped shirt on my sister looks like something Audrey Hepburn might have worn in *Roman Holiday*. I like to wear striped shirts with black slim-cut cropped pants, a trench, and slicked-back hair, à la Audrey in *Funny Face*.

STYLE

NOUN: *the way you adorn yourself within various contexts to express who you are uniquely, boldly, and unapologetically.*

You are

All too often, we look at a bag, a pair of pants, a pair of shoes, or a top and think, "I can't pull that off." I once bemoaned this phenomenon to a close friend. Her response was, "If you want to be a woman who wears X, just wear it!" So from that day on, I went for the item that I was afraid to wear, and allowed myself to fail, if it came to that. If I felt beautiful in it and just had to wear it differently than the mannequin, it was a win. If the item was a total bust, it went back to the store. The nature of style is that it's variable, and we have to give ourselves permission to try something out, even if we're not committed to it.

Can I be the friend who tells you to just wear the things that attract and intimidate you? Allow yourself to play and to change your mind. That piece you're afraid of could become your new favorite. Worthy of Wearing is not about looking super trendy or following the rules. Worthy of Wearing is about being comfortable in your own skin, from the inside out, and feeling proud of who God made you to be. Give yourself permission to invest in your self-worth, and your light will perpetually shine.

CHAPTER VII

THE
M-WORD:
MODESTY

M-WORD

modesty

For so many women, being modest means covering our bodies from the neck down to the wrists and ankles. It can be easy to overthink modesty, especially since there are no hard-and-fast rules on how to dress yourself as a woman of faith, other than Pope Pius XI's proposed list.[8] With this in mind, I wanted to provide some wisdom for you here.

Let's begin by defining the word *modesty*. The *Random House Dictionary* gives three definitions:

ONE

Freedom from vanity

TWO

Decency of behavior, speech, and dress

THREE

Simplicity and moderation

What do these definitions mean for our daily mode of dress? It all comes down to our intentions. "For where thy treasure is, there is thy heart also" (Matt. 6:21, Douay-Rheims). How we choose to clothe and adorn our bodies directly reflects our state in life, the context of our lifestyle and vocation (see chapter 9 for more on this topic), and the disposition of our soul. Our personal style is a reflection of our identity, inherent dignity, and femininity, and should authentically represent who we are to the people we meet and serve each day.

If we get dressed every day with the intention of being complimented, noticed, and preferred over others, then we are not free from vanity, whether we are wearing a form-fitting dress or a shapeless one that swallows our figure. In the Sermon on the Mount, Christ very clearly taught us not to become preoccupied with our appearance:

AND WHEN YOU FAST, BE NOT AS THE
HYPOCRITES, SAD. FOR THEY DISFIGURE
THEIR FACES, THAT THEY MAY APPEAR
UNTO MEN TO FAST. AMEN I SAY TO YOU,
THEY HAVE RECEIVED THEIR REWARD.
BUT THOU, WHEN THOU FASTEST ANOINT
THY HEAD, AND WASH THY FACE; THAT
THOU APPEAR NOT TO MEN TO FAST, BUT
TO THY FATHER WHO IS IN SECRET: AND
THY FATHER WHO SEETH IN SECRET, WILL
REPAY THEE. LAY NOT UP TO YOURSELVES
TREASURES ON EARTH: WHERE THE
RUST, AND MOTH CONSUME, AND WHERE
THIEVES BREAK THROUGH AND STEAL.
BUT LAY UP TO YOURSELVES TREASURES
IN HEAVEN: WHERE NEITHER THE RUST
NOR MOTH DOTH CONSUME, AND WHERE
THIEVES DO NOT BREAK THROUGH, NOR
STEAL.

MATT. 6:16–20, DOUAY-RHEIMS

We must wash our faces, clean our clothes, and dress ourselves for the day. When we wear clothing that suits us and makes us feel confident and comfortable, we can think of ourselves less and be more present to our daily calling. Vanity is like a stiff dance partner holding us in a waltz box step, which prevents our gaze from going beyond the stretch of our arms. Our focus becomes stuck on what others think of us and how we are perceived, and it taints our motivation such that we seek praise above the greatest good for our life. Falling into vanity quickly leads to other habits that detract from our inherent beauty, such as gossip, judging others, dishonesty, pride, and materialism. When we are free from vanity and have a joyful disposition because we acknowledge our worth as a gift from Christ, incredible things can happen for His glory. The strength that comes from dedicating each day to Our Lord will keep us from judging others and falling into hypocrisy.

"O SEARCH ME, GOD, AND KNOW
MY HEART. O TEST ME AND KNOW
MY THOUGHTS. SEE THAT I FOLLOW
NOT THE WRONG PATH AND LEAD
ME IN THE PATH OF LIFE ETERNAL."

PSALM 139 [138]:23–24
(GRAIL TRANSLATION)

How does the temptation to judge others ensnare us? Let's look at C. S. Lewis's *The Screwtape Letters,* a satirical collection of fictional letters from a demon to his protégé, containing advice on how to corrupt a soul (the "patient"):

> It matters very little, of course, what kind of people that next pew really contains. You may know one of them to be a great warrior on the Enemy's side. No matter. Your patient, thanks to Our Father Below, is a fool. Provided that any of those neighbours sing out of tune, or have boots that squeak, or double chins, or odd clothes, the patient will quite easily believe that their religion must therefore be somehow ridiculous. At his present stage, you see, he has an idea of "Christians" in his mind which he supposes to be spiritual but which, in fact, is largely pictorial. His mind is full of togas and sandals and armour and bare legs and the mere fact that the other people in church wear modern clothes is a real — though of course an unconscious — difficulty to him.[9]

Even more dangerous than simply comparing ourselves to others is the temptation to judge the hearts of other women based on the way they look. Only God knows a person's heart, which He has created for a specific purpose, as it is written in 1 Samuel 16:7: "And the Lord said to Samuel: Look not on his countenance, nor on the height of his stature: because I have rejected him, nor do I judge according to the look of man: for man seeth those things that appear, but the Lord beholdeth the heart" (Douay-Rheims). The Lord knows the intentions in our heart, whether we are making a big decision (such as which job to pursue or which person to marry) or a small decision (such as choosing to wear a dress instead of workout clothes). Judgments and comparisons distract us from the presence of God and often lead us to think badly of others and to feel discouraged. Instead, we should focus on our own intentions and strive to keep them pure and free from vanity.

The next aspects of modesty are simplicity, moderation, and decency of behavior, speech, and dress. All of them draw on the virtue of prudence, which, in cooperation with God's grace, helps us determine what is too much and what is not enough. Each woman will have a different rubric for discerning this based on her particular state in life, talents, preferences, and personality. Being simple, moderate, and decent means having a discerning heart and knowing our place as creatures who are made to love and serve God. This might look like standing up for the truth with courage or speaking delicately, not in a biting or cruel way.

When it comes to modesty, I like to keep in mind a simple question: "Is my behavior or my clothing distracting?" Our behavior and dress can amplify or detract from the wholeness of who we are in Christ: persons worthy of love, with unique gifts and talents, made to change hearts and spend eternity in Heaven. A low-cut dress can distract someone from your incredible talents, just as the way you gossip can distract someone from your virtue. Your unbridled anger might prevent someone from understanding the difficulties you face.

We can even distract ourselves by wearing clothing that misrepresents who we are or simply does not fit our body or state in life. Ever wear a skirt that's slightly too short, so your fingers keep grazing the hem to make sure it's in place? I have. In that moment, every word my boss said about our upcoming project sounded like mumbling because I was so distracted. And how about cutting your hair just like your best friend's, only to feel as though you're wearing a wig? I've been there. I hated going out in public with that mop because I couldn't figure out how to style it and still feel like myself. My haircut seemed to be wearing me, instead of the other way around.

So what counts as "distracting"? It varies, based on your body type, age, vocation, and state in life. A cartwheeling, pirouetting seven-year-old, a twenty-seven-year-old new mother, and a fifty-seven-year-old professional will all practice modesty differently. The same goes for women who are called to be rooted in the home, women who are called to religious life, and women who are called to live in the public eye, whether through ministry, media, business, or creative pursuits. Even the devotions by which Christ has invited us to love Him can shape how we practice modesty. Some women may feel called to wear a veil at Mass or to follow Marian modesty guidelines, dressing themselves the way the Blessed Mother and many other saints did.

Other women feel called to wear the latest fashions and to be approachable, integrated members of their community. For the record, I know some women who wear a veil at Mass and wear the latest fashions. Again, it is up to each woman's discernment to hear where Christ is calling her and to live out that calling with authenticity, gusto, and obedience.

While it would be convenient to have an objective list of modesty rules that all women should follow, strict guidelines do us a disservice, as we are all unique, with specific missions that Christ calls us to fulfill. Let's not scrupulously debate the ideal thickness of a tank-top strap, or whether skirts should hit above, at, or below the knee. Instead, let's learn how our clothes drape our body, how they move when we walk, sit, or bend over. Ultimately, feeling comfortable, free to move, and present to those we see every day is an expression of modesty.

One tip I always recommend is to take your clothing for a test drive before wearing it out or while hosting friends in your home. Wiggle in it! How do you feel when you sit, stand, and bend over? Can you bend over to tie your shoe or pick something up from the floor without exposing yourself (whether because the top falls out or the bottom rides up)? When you walk, does the garment trip you, because it's too long? Does it have a loose button or wonky zipper? Do you need smoothing undergarments to help the fabric drape as it was designed, or maybe an undergarment that is less visible? Does the garment look best when ironed, or is it made of wash-and-wear fabric? When light shines, can you see through the garment? Can you raise your arms up high or reach out for a hug without feeling tightness across your shoulders or underarms? Does the fabric open up when you walk or sit (this is especially important for wrap dresses and clothing with slits)? Does the waist cinch your hips and cut them in half (creating what some call a muffin top), or are there creases across the tops of your thighs and your crotch area? If the answer is yes to any of these questions, try sizing up, purchasing undergarments that smooth and cover your bottom half, or taking your garment to a tailor to adjust too-deep necklines, too-long hems, or loose bodices.

In summary, a modest wardrobe isn't one that sacrifices modernity or stylishness, but simply one that fits your state in life, represents your God-given dignity, and highlights your natural beauty. When you dress modestly, you reveal your intentionality and self-worth, eliciting respect from others. My hope is that practicing modesty will help you feel empowered.

CHAPTER VIII

FIRST IMPRESSIONS AND EVANGELIZATION

CHAPTER SEVEN

FIRST *impressions*

&EVANGELIZATION

Did you know

it takes us only seven seconds to form a first impression of someone? The way you present yourself in that sliver of time is crucial. Imagine you have only seven seconds to get your dream job, meet your future best friend or spouse, or find a business partner who can bring your dreams to life. What part of your story would you want to share with your clothing? Maybe you'd like to share your practicality, decisiveness, and attention to detail, so you wear perfectly tailored pieces in neutral colors with the daintiest jewelry. Maybe you'd share your colorful personality by wearing eye-catching hues with sharp silhouettes and playful accessories. Or maybe you'd wear pieces from an era you love.

Clothing gives us an opportunity to connect with others on matters of the heart. Simply calling out "I love your shoes!" as you pass by can spark a conversation that leads to so much more. After my first few weeks of working in the top floor showroom of a New York designer, a girl my age was hired. The first thing I noticed about her was her jet-black, wiry, blunt cut hair, which brushed her shoulders as she walked. Like me, she wore a lot of black, but with some twists: lace-up boots, fishnet tights, chain details, black eyeliner, and a few face piercings. She was quiet and avoided eye contact, and I was ready to make a new friend. Fashion showrooms are notoriously quiet! As I showed her around and gave her the rundown on our duties, I found a way to connect with her. I asked her where she'd bought her killer boots, which led to a discussion on where she'd grown up in Queens, New York. She liked my red lipstick and asked me where I'd gotten my silky black maxi skirt. We discovered that we spoke similar style languages and shared a deep love for New York City.

Over the months that we worked together, a bond formed. We ate lunch together every day, silently shot each other looks of support across the showroom during stressful times, and huddled together in the endless racks of clothes to chat while on break. We danced and danced during a Fashion Week after-party. But we could not have been more different. She shared difficult parts of her childhood with me — things I never faced — and I greatly admired her perseverance and grit. She also revealed that after years of parochial school, she had left the Catholic Faith and embraced agnosticism. She asked me why I still believed, and I responded vulnerably. In our shared cubicle in the executive sales office, we had many whispered conversations about faith, family, dreams, and the existence of God. Though we held opposing beliefs, our mutual respect and a few other commonalities made many of our discussions really powerful, to say the least. This wonderful connection wouldn't have been made without our shared love of style.

A few years later, I was riding the subway and saw from behind a woman with wiry jet-black hair and a red plaid miniskirt. It was her. My arm slid down the rail toward where she stood, and we caught up on the shuttle between Grand Central and Times Square. You never know why God brings certain people into and out of your life, often by chance, and sometimes only for a short time. As women, we can't deny how our personal appearance can often bridge a connection that otherwise wouldn't have begun. Our style allows us to make the most of the seven seconds we have to make a first impression.

When used as a manifestation of our interior life, our appearance can be a tool for evangelization. Think about God's creation: a peach-colored sunrise, snow-capped mountains, rushing waterfalls, fields of sunflowers. Each one sparks such surprise and awe that our hearts intuitively know it could not have been man-made. Someone who has never heard of the one true God may intuit His existence from the wonders of Mother Nature. Our clothing can inspire the same surprise and wonder not only in us but also in those we encounter.

Have you heard of St. Bernadette and the story of how the Blessed Virgin Mary appeared to her? The Mother of God revealed herself in all her beauty and greeted the young girl with a smile. When the authorities, who were convinced the apparitions were a hoax, questioned Bernadette, she said the woman who appeared to her was surrounded by a white light. When Bernadette was asked to clarify what the lady looked like, she recalled that the Virgin Mary was more beautiful than the town's most recent bride, who was notably stunning. The townspeople erupted in disbelief!

In a homily at Lourdes, France, where Our Lady appeared to St. Bernadette, Pope Emeritus Benedict XVI said: "A simple young girl from Lourdes, Bernadette Soubirous, saw a light, and in this light she saw a young lady who was 'beautiful, more beautiful than any other.' This woman addressed her with kindness and gentleness, with respect and trust.… It is hardly surprising that Mary should be beautiful." He added that Mary gives us an example of how clothing ourselves with Christ allows us to share His hope and goodness with the world: "Mary left death behind her; she is entirely re-clothed with life, the life of her Son, the risen Christ. She is thus the sign of the victory of love, of good and of God, giving our world the hope that it needs."[10]

We know, too, that Our Lady dresses in the same manner as those to whom she appears. To St. Juan Diego, an Aztec convert to Catholicism, Our Lady of Guadalupe appeared as an Aztec princess. If our way of dressing and caring for our body were of no importance, those blessed with visions of the Mother of Divine Grace would pay little attention to the details of her physical appearance. Rather, our clothing, our conduct, and the way we address others directly represent what is in our heart. Our contagious joy can be a cause for hope, just as displays of misery can instill despair in those we encounter.

How dangerous it can be to misrepresent who we are and what we believe, to wear a facade of goodness while neglecting our interior life. When we fall into hypocrisy, we turn our backs on Christ, and in serious cases, we cause scandal or confusion. Instead, we should imitate Our Lady, the handmaid of the Lord, who clothed herself with the life of Christ and became a living temple of the Holy Spirit.

> *He*
> *will transform*
> *us in*
> *flames of love.*

— ST. THÉRÈSE OF LISIEUX

Christ calls us to reveal the light of His love in our every action. Even the way we act, move, and dress is a form of evangelization. Rather than dressing to meet someone else's standards or expectations, we dress to express our identity as Christian women. We use personal style to celebrate our God-given beauty and to reflect Christ, our Creator and Savior. Furthermore, the way we dress directly affects the souls God puts in our path. It is up to us to be authentic Christians and to make our way of life look as attractive on the outside as it is on the inside.

Be brave with who you are and what you wear! You might inspire someone else to do the same. Imagine the domino effect you could create by confidently harnessing the goodness God placed in your heart and sharing His love with the world.

You don't have to wait for a special occasion to dress in a way that makes you feel and look lovely. When we feel good, we can serve others freely, focusing more on them and less on ourselves. If we do "small things with great love" for ourselves, we can extend that love to others. By contrast, when we wear clothes that don't reflect who we are, we may cause others to misunderstand us, which often makes us feel lonely. That's why it's important for us to understand who God created us to be, so we can dress accordingly and live authentically the gorgeous life He has planned for us.

"

TO LIVE CHRISTIAN *love*, MEANS AT THE SAME TIME TO
INTRODUCE *God's light into the world* AND TO POINT OUT
its true source. SAINT LEO THE GREAT WRITES: 'WHOEVER,
IN FACT, LIVES A *holy* AND *chaste* LIFE IN THE CHURCH,
WHOEVER SETS HIS MIND ON THINGS THAT ARE *above*, NOT
ON THINGS THAT ARE ON EARTH (CF. COL 3:2), IN A CERTAIN
WAY RESEMBLES *heavenly light*; AS LONG AS HE HIMSELF
OBSERVES THE BRILLIANCE OF A HOLY LIFE, HE SHOWS TO
MANY, LIKE A STAR, *the path that leads to God'* (SERMON
III:5).

HOMILY OF HIS HOLINESS BENEDICT XVI, LOURDES,
ROSARY SQUARE, SEPTEMBER 13, 2008.

NATALIE PETERS

Independent Art Scholar

HOW WOULD YOU DESCRIBE YOUR STYLE IN THREE TO FIVE WORDS?

Eclectic, feminine, streamlined.

HOW DO YOUR VOCATION AND LIFESTYLE TRANSLATE TO WHAT YOU WEAR?

I'm a wife and I work from home, so I keep things comfortable, but pulled together. When I take the extra time to get ready each day, I feel beautiful for my spouse and more confident as I approach my work. It sets the tone for my day. I'm a hands-on person, so I'm regularly getting into projects at the house. But I don't believe in "grungy work clothes." Most tasks can be done while wearing something nice. Laundry is inevitable in life, so why not wear something nice?

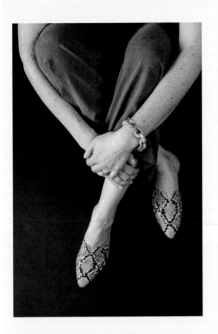

I love subtle patterns that are proportionate to my size, small florals, and simple stripes. And my favorite silhouettes are streamlined — things that drape easily and have movement. When I was growing up, I was embarrassed to be shaped like a Skipper Barbie doll (ha!) until I realized many of my favorite actresses in old movies also had very little curve. So I embraced it!

WHAT IS THE BEST ITEM YOU'VE EVER SCORED WHILE SHOPPING?

My wedding shoes: designer satin kitten heels. They rang up for one penny!

WHAT MOTIVATES YOU WHEN YOU GET DRESSED?

The instant feeling I have when I'm put together for that day: I feel elevated and ready to serve in my mission. I'm hooked on that feeling.

WHAT IS ONE STYLE MISTAKE YOU WISH YOU HADN'T MADE?

Wearing colors on-trend rather than those that suited me. That was a short, but terrible phase.

WHERE DO YOU FIND INSPIRATION FOR HOW YOU DRESS?

Art and nature, color, and texture are very inspiring to me. Also, old movies.

WHAT IS THE MOST TREASURED PIECE IN YOUR CLOSET?

My yellow tweed jacket. It's very Jackie O. I bought it back in college when I was shopping with my dad. He pulled it off the rack and said: "Now that's perfect. This will never go out of style. You'll wear this forever." And he was right. I always think of him when I see it, and it's a reminder to invest in a unique item even when it seems "impractical."

WHAT ARE YOUR FAVORITE FABRICS, PATTERNS, OR SILHOUETTES TO WEAR, AND WHY?

I love natural fibers — cotton blends, linen, silk, and wool. They're so beautiful, last longer, and look more elegant than synthetics.

WHAT IS YOUR CONFIDENCE OUTFIT?

Anything formal. I feel comfortab and confident.

NAME THREE WOMEN (FICTIONAL OR REAL) WHOSE STYLE INSPIRES YOUR OWN.

Myrna Loy, Katharine Hepburn, Emma Stone.

IF YOU COULD WEAR ANY SINGLE PAIR OF SHOES FOR THE REST OF YOUR LIFE, WHAT WOULD YOU PICK?

Sandals. I hate socks.

WHAT IS YOUR FAVORITE ACCESSORY?

Bracelets.

HOW LONG AGO DID YOU EMBRACE AND FEEL CONFIDENT WITH YOUR PERSONAL STYLE?

I think style and confidence ha seasons in life. You have to ke working at them both as you gr and change. I recently rediscover my own, and it's been fun to ma space to get to know myself anew.

WHAT IS YOUR ADVICE FOR
A WOMAN WHO DOESN'T FEEL
WORTHY OF WEARING?

*Fake it till you make it. Take the
extra time to put yourself together
even if you don't believe it, don't
feel it, and very soon you will start
to feel inside how you appear on the
outside. You will come to see that you
are, indeed, truly worthy.*

WHAT IS ONE MAKEUP ITEM
YOU CAN'T LIVE WITHOUT?

Mascara!

FAVORITE SEASON TO DRESS
FOR?

Spring.

RAPID FIRE ROUND

HEELS, FLATS, OR SNEAKERS?	*FLATS*
COFFEE, TEA, OR WATER WITH LEMON?	*COFFEE*
SALTY SNACKS OR SWEET DESSERT?	*SALTY*
BLAZER OR CARDIGAN?	*BLAZER*
DRESS OR TROUSERS?	*DRESS*
MASCARA OR LIPSTICK?	*MASCARA*
CHUNKY OR DAINTY JEWELRY?	*CHUNKY*
SHORTER HAIR OR LONGER HAIR?	*LONGER*
BRIGHT COLORS OR NEUTRALS?	*COLORS*
PRINTS OR SOLIDS?	*PRINTS*

MARY LENABURG

Author and Speaker

HOW WOULD YOU DESCRIBE YOUR STYLE IN THREE TO FIVE WORDS?
Bold, feminine, classic and sassy, heavy on the accessories.

HOW DO YOUR VOCATION AND LIFESTYLE TRANSLATE TO WHAT YOU WEAR?
It's changed over the years. When my kids were little, there were lots of jeans and sweatpants. Now it's tailored trousers, dresses, and a more put-together look.

WHERE DO YOU FIND INSPIRATION FOR HOW YOU DRESS?

I love looking at fashion magazines or Pinterest for inspiration. So many fabulous ideas. People-watching is fun as well.

WHAT IS THE MOST TREASURED PIECE IN YOUR CLOSET?

I have a navy blue midi dress inspired by Audrey Hepburn, [with a] full skirt and a bateau neckline. It's so flattering on my plus-size figure. I feel like a million dollars in that dress.

WHAT ARE YOUR FAVORITE FABRICS, PATTERNS, OR SILHOUETTES TO WEAR, AND WHY?

I have never met a tunic blouse and a skinny jean I have not loved. I am plus-size with a very long torso, so it can be a struggle to find something that's long enough. I am big on bold colors and pattern mixing as well. You would never use the word boring when describing my wardrobe.

WHAT IS THE BEST ITEM YOU'VE EVER SCORED WHILE SHOPPING?

A cashmere dress coat for under one hundred dollars. It was beautiful.

WHAT MOTIVATES YOU WHEN YOU GET DRESSED?

I learned early in life that you dress for the day you wish to have, so I do, down to the choice of makeup and accessories.

WHAT IS ONE STYLE MISTAKE YOU WISH YOU HADN'T MADE?

Farrah Fawcett hair my freshman year of high school, along with the frosty blue eyeshadow. Yikes! Bad choice.

WHAT IS YOUR CONFIDENCE OUTFIT?

I love wearing a dress with a jacket, a fabulous pair of statement earrings, and colorful shoes. It's feminine, with a side of masculine tailoring. Works beautifully.

NAME THREE WOMEN (FICTIONAL OR REAL) WHOSE STYLE INSPIRES YOUR OWN.

Grace Kelly, Kate Middleton, and Sarah Jessica Parker.

IF YOU COULD WEAR ANY SINGLE PAIR OF SHOES FOR THE REST OF YOUR LIFE, WHAT WOULD YOU PICK?

My leopard-print pumps.

WHAT IS YOUR FAVORITE ACCESSORY?

Hands down, a spectacular statement earring.

WHAT IS YOUR ADVICE FOR A WOMAN WHO DOESN'T FEEL WORTHY OF WEARING?

Confidence comes when we know our worth. You are a beautiful daughter of God, made in His image and likeness. Receive His love. It's the best gift He could ever give you. Take it in and hold your head high. You honor His sacrifice on the Cross when you honor your worth.

WHAT IS ONE MAKEUP ITEM YOU CAN'T LIVE WITHOUT?

Lip gloss.

FAVORITE SEASON TO DRESS FOR?

Definitely fall. The sweaters, boots, scarves . . . I love it all!

RAPID FIRE ROUND

HEELS, FLATS, OR SNEAKERS?
  BALLET FLATS.

COFFEE, TEA, OR WATER WITH LEMON?
  IS THAT EVEN A QUESTION? COFFEE, ALWAYS.

SALTY SNACKS OR SWEET DESSERT?
  HOW ABOUT A SALTY-SWEET SNACK, LIKE CHOCOLATE-COVERED PRETZELS. SO GOOD.

BLAZER OR CARDIGAN?
  CARDIGAN.

DRESS OR TROUSERS?
  DRESS

MASCARA OR LIPSTICK?
  BOTH!

CHUNKY OR DAINTY JEWELRY?
  CHUNKY.

SHORTER HAIR OR LONGER HAIR?
  SHORTER HAIR.

BRIGHT COLORS OR NEUTRALS?
  THE BRIGHTER, THE BETTER.

PRINTS OR SOLIDS?
  PRINTS.

REAGAN ANTONIO

Homemaker

HOW WOULD YOU DESCRIBE YOUR STYLE IN THREE TO FIVE WORDS?

Bold, easy, fun staples.

HOW DO YOUR VOCATION AND LIFESTYLE TRANSLATE TO WHAT YOU WEAR?

I'm a homemaker! I'm a mother and a wife. I love style — especially clothing and interior design. Our fulfillment here on earth is the best worship we can give God, and it involves discerning who He created us to be, and then cooperating with that vision as fully as possible. So the way I dress should make me feel

I get more attached to my earrings than my clothes, maybe because growing up in Michigan's seasons put a term limit on every outfit! But right now, there's a silver, 100 percent silk skirt that I found new with tags at a thrift store for a fraction of the price, and a size or two up from my normal size. My baby bump is almost big enough for the perfect fit, and it is so wonderful to have a treasured piece of clothing that depends on my changing body to . . . change! I can't wait for my bump to grow so I can enjoy this special skirt.

WHAT ARE YOUR FAVORITE FABRICS, PATTERNS, OR SILHOUETTES TO WEAR, AND WHY?

Straight-leg pants! They're so feminine and balanced, accentuating a woman's hips and ankles by giving them some room to breathe. Plus, you never have to worry about a fashion faux pas from a big gust of wind when you're wearing pants! And I love classic styles in fun prints — like a houndstooth turtleneck, or a cardigan with glitter thread woven through it, or a plaid wool blazer. I love to accentuate a wardrobe of neutrals (grays, blacks, whites and creams, tans, and cheetah print) with rich jewel tones — a pair of emerald block heels, or aquamarine tassel earrings, or a pattern that mixes sapphire blue with those neutrals I mentioned.

WHAT IS THE BEST ITEM YOU'VE EVER SCORED WHILE SHOPPING?

Once, I found this "pants-skirt" on the clearance rack at Anthropologie for hundreds of dollars off. Straight-leg, copper silk pants were covered by sheer, super glittery, asymmetrical gold-copper layers of a skirt. Depending on the angle, I was either wearing a skirt or a pair of pants. They were the best holiday "wow" piece. Sadly, they disappeared during one of my many college moves, and I've never tracked them down. Their memory lives on, though!

WHAT MOTIVATES YOU WHEN YOU GET DRESSED?

It's almost the other way around — getting dressed motivates me! Putting together an outfit and deciding how I do my eyeshadow in the morning starts my day with a creative outlet that I find so energizing. When picking out an outfit is more draining than exciting, I know it's time to get rid of some clothes — having too much is almost always the culprit when I have "absolutely nothing to wear"! Either that or it's time to do some laundry.

beautiful (Because I am a bride! My husband's and my God's), but it also needs to support those other parts of my vocation. So buy those sparkly pants — did you notice they have some stretch? They capture the beauty God put uniquely on my heart, and I can wipe counters, fold laundry, cook dinner, [and] play on the floor with a baby in them. Another big reminder: God gave us washing machines. If you only wear clothes because "it's okay to get them dirty," you're going to look like a dirty hamper. Wear beautiful clothes, and then wash them when life happens. Rather than compromise on style, compromise on fabrics that are easier to take care of.

WHERE DO YOU FIND INSPIRATION FOR HOW YOU DRESS?

I love seeing what other women wear (and how). New York street style inspires me big time — I especially love digging through Fashion Week snapshots for all the street style.

WHAT IS THE MOST TREASURED PIECE IN YOUR CLOSET?

WHAT IS ONE STYLE MISTAKE YOU WISH YOU HADN'T MADE?

Ultimately, even though I have some truly cringeworthy outfits (and pictures for evidence!), I'm grateful for all of my "phases" of style because they helped me figure out what's "me," and what's "me trying to fit in." I arrived on my college campus in a full-blown bohemian phase — wide headbands, mismatched earrings up both earlobes, flowy dresses, and clean skin. I ended up ditching it because I didn't feel like a "grown-up," and it definitely didn't transfer well to a traditional workplace dress code. In high school, I went through a preppy phase, but it always looked frumpy because I'd wear the preppy clothes without the styled hair and makeup to complete the look. It's easy to exclude everything except our clothes from our understanding of style, but true style is all about integration — how do the clothes, shoes, accessories, hair, and makeup I choose for myself tell the story of the kind of woman I am?

WHAT IS YOUR CONFIDENCE OUTFIT?

Real denim jeans (the no-stretch high waist even makes me stand up taller!), a button-down shirt with the sleeves rolled a few times for a more relaxed look, and a pair of chunky heels.

NAME THREE WOMEN (FICTIONAL OR REAL) WHOSE STYLE INSPIRES YOUR OWN.

01.

Lots of fashion bloggers. Laura Wills [of The Fashion Bug*] is one of my very favorite fashion bloggers because she is the best at integrating her regular wardrobe and style with her maternity style. I get so much inspiration from her glam-mama outfits!*

02.

My mom — especially the photos of her when she was my age. While certain out-dated patterns or silhouettes make me giggle, I can't tell you how many times I've spotted a killer pair of jeans in a yearbook of my mom's and begged for them to be folded up in a corner of her closet somewhere. While none of her amazing 1980s jeans made it, certain old college sweatshirts are still going strong. It makes me think about the clothes I choose to invest in for myself. Would my daughter want to wear this someday? Could it stand the test of time if I wanted it to? Do I carry myself in a way that my daughters and granddaughters will be able to recognize in photos someday — the same joy, the same spirit, the same femininity?

03.

St. Gianna Molla — not because of any particular outfit of hers, but because the way she dressed told the story of who she was: a strong, holy woman vibrantly living out her faith through her vocation as a doctor, a wife, and a mother. She didn't dress as a "saint"; she dressed exactly for her time and for the vocation God gave her. Sometimes I watch women fall into the trap of thinking they need to dress like a saint they love from the 1800s in order to be saintly themselves. No, no: our sainthood is here and now. Dress here and now! Sanctify the time and the place that God has asked of you — not one hundred years ago or one thousand miles away. Right where you are. Right now.

IF YOU COULD WEAR ANY SINGLE PAIR OF SHOES FOR THE REST OF YOUR LIFE, WHAT WOULD YOU PICK?

Lately, spending more time at home, I've been living out of my slippers. They have a fur edge around the ankle that makes them look a little bit fancy, and I hate walking around barefoot with cold toes! But for "real" shoes, I have a few different block heels that are truly so versatile, like the bright red open-toed sandals with a modest block heel and the cutest suede knot across the top of the foot. They slip on, are comfortable, and perfect every outfit from jeans and a button-down for a night out to your prettiest Sunday dress.

WHAT IS YOUR FAVORITE ACCESSORY?

Simple, classic, bold statement pieces . . . a watch, a chunky gold chain bracelet (the gold is classic, but the chunk is a bold twist), or a pair of gold hoop earrings.

HOW LONG AGO DID YOU EMBRACE AND FEEL CONFIDENT WITH YOUR PERSONAL STYLE?

A move to D.C. for a semester on an extremely tight budget meant everything I owned for that semester — bedding, wardrobe, textbooks — had to fit into my free bags [for the flight]. It forced me to do a massive detox of my wardrobe. I got rid of nearly two-thirds of my wardrobe. I had to decide what kind of woman I wanted to look like to the strangers I passed on the sidewalks. Basics like button-downs can be dressed up for work with slacks and down for parties with jeans. Nice shoes can be worn to work or to the grocery store (with a solid pair of sneakers for getting around!), and so on. The style I nailed down halfway through college hasn't really changed much. I love basics, a loyal pair of jeans, bold accessories, and an easy, pulled-together look.

WHAT IS YOUR ADVICE FOR A WOMAN WHO DOESN'T FEEL WORTHY OF WEARING?

Every single soul was created by God with a particular mission and vocation for the Kingdom. There are no replacements or "subs." Dive into the unique interests, passions, and beauties that God has given to you in particular, because the Kingdom grows brighter when we become more wholly ourselves as women — not more wholly like the woman next to us or who we think we need to be. We need to be ourselves. The more we become ourselves, the more we become the image of God.

"How much has the Lord entrusted to us? How many graces has He conferred on others as a result of our lives? How many people are depending on my own correspondence with grace? . . . Each man and each woman serve as soldiers commissioned by God to guard a part of his fortress of the Universe. Some soldiers are stationed on the walls, others in the interior of the castle. Everyone needs to be faithful to his duty and assignment. No one can abandon their post. If this were to happen, then the fortress would be exposed to the assaults of hell."[11]

WHAT IS ONE MAKEUP ITEM YOU CAN'T LIVE WITHOUT?

My brow pencil. Eyebrows frame the face. I don't feel dressed without "putting on" my eyebrows! If I am so pressed for time I can only choose one makeup item, I'll put on brows first. Then mascara, and then a quick-swipe statement lip for the easiest French-girl look.

FAVORITE SEASON TO DRESS FOR?

Fall-winter. I love the flexibility that comes with layers — it feels like there are more options to play around with. Also, a big fluffy coat and some glam sunglasses can make anything look fabulous (even leggings).

RAPID FIRE ROUND

HEELS, FLATS, OR SNEAKERS?

A CHUNKY BLOCK HEEL WHEN IT'S WARM AND SHINY LUG-SOLE BOOTS WHEN THE TEMPS DROP.

COFFEE, TEA, OR WATER WITH LEMON?

COFFEE. FOREVER.

SALTY SNACKS OR SWEET DESSERT?

SALTY (UNLESS IT'S DARK CHOCOLATE).

BLAZER OR CARDIGAN?

BLAZER.

DRESS OR TROUSERS?

TROUSERS.

MASCARA OR LIPSTICK?

LASHES FOR DAYS.

CHUNKY OR DAINTY JEWELRY?

CHUNKY!

SHORTER HAIR OR LONGER HAIR?

LONGER.

BRIGHT COLORS OR NEUTRALS?

NEUTRALS.

PRINTS OR SOLIDS?

PRINTS.

HOW TO
CURATE

three

A WORTHY
WARDROBE

DRESS FOR THIS SEASON

dress

FOR

this

SEASON

At least fifty times over the course of my life, I have stared at my closet, nearly empty because its contents lay in piles on my bed, and thought, "I have nothing to wear." Maybe you've had similar experiences. You have plenty of clothes, but none of them make you feel authentic, stylish, and peaceful. This phenomenon, which we all face at one point or another, tends to make us late for work, school, or wherever we're going. When we do arrive, we often feel uncomfortable, self-conscious, and distracted — and that's all before lunch. How can we carry out the mission God has given us when we lose so much time going through piles of clothing every other day and getting caught up in the chaos of insecurity, confusion, and lack of fulfillment?

Sifting through a cluttered closet is tiresome, and it's hard to keep track of the items and styles you really love. Our wardrobes accumulate excess with little effort. Maybe an older sister passed down a dress she's grown tired of, or a relative gave you a scarf you never want to wear, no matter how many times you pull it out of the drawer. Likewise, clearance-rack prices are often too good to pass up, but the items never quite make sense with the rest of your wardrobe because you bought them on impulse, without a plan. You may even have two or three of the same item, but not enough of your uniform basics — you know, those things you wear week in and week out that always seem to be in the dirty laundry pile. The end result of all this clutter is a mismatched selection of trendy or ill-fitting pieces that completely misrepresent who you are or what season you're in. Seasons may include a time in your life, such as your college years, or a time of year, such as fall. Either way, they are temporary. Lifestyle shifts happen all the time, sometimes weekly or monthly depending on your state in life, and unexpected things come our way, often bringing physical changes with them. Pregnancy, menopause, health challenges, stress, loss, hormonal changes, and even medications can cause our figure to fluctuate, and we have to adjust accordingly. Some of us embrace these changes, and some of us have difficulty with them. Regardless of how you respond, it's all too easy to cling to past seasons — for example, by wearing the same clothes you wore in college fifteen years after graduation. But when we cling to what has passed, we miss the opportunity to embrace a new phase of life.

I cannot stress enough how important it is to remember that new seasons in life, and in weather, require small tweaks in your clothing. We are ever growing and ever changing, and our style should reflect that. Something in your closet that you love right now might be your least favorite item next year. Keep these things in mind and allow yourself to be flexible. You don't have to be a slave to trends, but you have to allow yourself the space to always be open to new things. Personal style is dynamic, not static!

Women who have given birth know this truth well. From the moment of conception, our bodies are not our own. They must change to accommodate the new life growing within us. Our hips widen, stretch marks appear, and the shape of our body changes. We lose hair and gain melasma. Some of us even grow a shoe size!

Our bodies continue to change throughout pregnancy and into the postpartum period. Since gestation takes nine months, a woman's body also needs nine months, and I would argue a full year, to adjust to nurturing her baby after birth. As time for ourselves takes a hit, including time for our self-care habits, we have to find a new groove. We might need to adjust to a new type of clothing that suits our role as a mother, and possibly in a different size than we're used to. Does that mean our pre-pregnancy clothes will never fit again? No; however, it is important to give ourselves space to adjust, so we can honor the strength our bodies have shown in bearing children.

True story: I recently messaged my sister, "I have no idea what size my body will be next year." I am writing this book after having a baby. Planning for my brother's wedding a few seasons from now feels like walking in the dark. But my changing body is part of my vocation. The pressure so many mothers face to get their body "back," as if pregnancy took it away, diminishes the beauty of motherhood. Not only our bellies but also our hearts expand with each of our children. Motherhood, for those of us called to it, is our pathway to Heaven. Accepting a higher number on the scale, sagging skin, and wider hips may require us to surrender with humility, but these changes are the very signs that we have co-created life with Our Lord. They testify to the future generations we have brought into the world. Our job as mothers is noble, requiring a true death to self. If we can help one another to see the beauty in the changes in our bodies, instead of wearing worn-out stretchy pants and fad-dieting until our old clothes fit again, we could encourage more women to see that motherhood, and all the changes it brings to our lives, is a divine gift.

Whether expected or unexpected, lifestyle changes can be difficult to rebound from. As we ride the wave of life, we should make time to reflect on our needs for each new season and make practical adjustments where necessary. Our needs fall into three categories:

SPIRITUAL NEEDS: our prayer routine, what we read for spiritual nourishment, how much time we make for silence in our day, and how often we receive the sacraments and seek support in spiritual direction.

EMOTIONAL NEEDS: how much time we dedicate to our relationships and communities, and how often we make space for self-expression, creativity, and reflection.

PHYSICAL NEEDS: how how we dress, care for our skin and our body, maintain hygiene, and prioritize exercise, rest, and nutrition.

"Each woman who lives in the light of eternity can fulfill her vocation."

ST. TERESA BENEDICTA OF THE CROSS

Make time to reevaluate these three areas. What needs attention? What are the hopes you can make into habits? For many years, I idealized a certain way of living, but often felt at a loss as to how to make it part of my life. Then, I learned about what James Clear, author of the book *Atomic Habits*, calls "habit stacking." Habit stacking is a way of accomplishing tasks by making them dependent on each other's completion. For example, rather than walking straight to the coffee pot every morning, I challenged myself to drink two glasses of water while the water for my coffee came to a boil. And before enjoying my first sip of coffee, I had to be seated in place for my Magnificat morning prayer routine. Once I began stacking these habits, making coffee was no longer about simply guzzling caffeine; it was the foundation of a ritual that created simplicity and consistency in my life. I love using this system as I go through my day. How can you use habit stacking to begin living the life you hope for?

THE DAILY GRIND

Whether or not you are "seen" in public or at home every day has nothing to do with how worthy you are to dress in a way that makes you feel fantastic. You are worthy of wearing an outfit that puts you in touch with your dignity, just for your own simple enjoyment. It's a mood-lifter! Life is too short not to give dressing well a try. Watch your productivity soar, smiles bubble up without effort, and dreams begin to take root.

Wearing something beautiful witnesses to the beauty God gave you. Think of the inside of a church — the house of God. The altar is draped with delicate lace. There are flowers and plants to show the beauty of creation. Gold is paired with carved wood and marble, while fleur-de-lis and star motifs dazzle overhead. Have you ever seen the Cathedral of Santa Maria del Fiore in Florence or St. Patrick's Cathedral in Manhattan? Even the stone facade and external staircases and statues are a manifestation of the material and spiritual beauty that is inside.

Muse over what your current season is, taking into consideration both your vocation and your physical location, so you can create the starting point of your Worthy Wardrobe.

The contexts in which we live often dictate what is practical, useful, and beneficial for our day-to-day. Remember, a woman who lives in Alaska will have a different wardrobe for December than a woman who lives in South Carolina. A woman who lives in a busy city has different day-to-day clothing needs than a woman who homesteads on her family's farm. The term casual wear can have two entirely different definitions depending on where you live and where you are called. That is exactly why I can't list Ten Things You Need Right Now, as many magazines do, because we all have different needs, contexts, and vocations.

What I can do is give you a few ideas on how to dress for your state in life. By no means is every vocation included here, but I hope this gives you a place to start.

Generally, we have both informal and formal roles. We might need to dress formally on the weekdays and casually on the weekends, or maybe vice versa. And we all need a few go-to outfits saved just for the Sabbath! The following suggestions will help you identify where your daily contexts fall, so you can work your clothes into your life accordingly.

IF YOU HAVE ROLES WITH

AN INFORMAL DRESS CODE,

SUCH AS STUDENT, TEACHER, ATHLETE,
MISSIONARY, ARTIST OR CREATIVE,
MOTHER, OR CAREGIVER:

Try finding items that are easy to maneuver in, don't require readjustment with every movement, and can be easily laundered (because stains happen). Fabrics that breathe well and maybe even have a slight stretch will move with you throughout the day. Jeans with any top, a tunic with opaque leggings, a sweater with cropped skinny pants, or a comfortable dress or skirt combo can be the foundation of your daily style. You can personalize this basic look with the colors, prints, and silhouettes you love.

A FORMAL
DRESS CODE,

SUCH AS A JOB IN THE CORPORATE, FINANCIAL,
MEDICAL, NONPROFIT, GOVERNMENT, LAW, OR REAL
ESTATE SECTOR:

Look for tailored pieces that complement your shape without being too loose or too tight (or too short or too low). Items that can be worn from day to night, such as suits, sheath dresses, knitwear sets, blouses, and pencil skirts in neutral tones are easy to mix and match. You can wear these pieces over and over again without looking like it. Closed-toe shoes, dressed-up outerwear, colored blouses, and accessories are where you can have some fun and personalize your look.

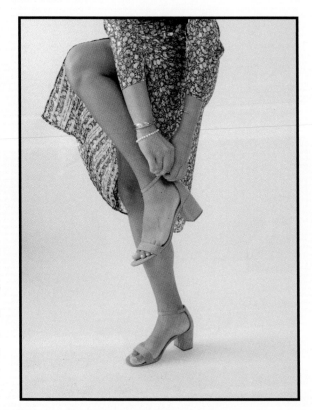

Remember the term *Sunday best?* Sunday has traditionally been the one day every week for when we mend, press, and lay out our very best clothes ahead of time. We begin preparing for Holy Mass the night before. But why?

Because when we walk inside a church, we are in God's house — a place of prayer and worship. And when we walk into a Catholic church, we are in the presence of the Holy Eucharist, the presence of Our Lord. Our simple human intellect can barely comprehend what it truly means to be in the presence of the one true God. St. Jean-Marie Vianney simply stated, "If we really understood the Mass, we would die of joy." We can't fully understand the profound gift of attending Holy Mass. If we did, we would likely faint before ever approaching the altar to receive Holy Communion.

Our lack of awareness of the significance of Mass is sometimes reflected in how we behave and dress. Casual clothing and casual culture go hand in hand, and you may notice that most people wear the same clothes at church that they wear at the supermarket or on the soccer field. I myself have done this many times. In fact, this has become commonplace in many parishes across America. But as my understanding of Whom I was worshipping at Mass grew, I began to want to set aside something special just for Him. Dressing up reminded me that I was entering a different context, and I needed to be focused on Christ, not myself or other worshippers. If I believed that the Mass was a meeting of Heaven and earth, why wouldn't I dress accordingly?

PICNIC, WOULD YOU WEAR A COCKTAIL DRESS?

INTERVIEWER GO ON WITH QUESTIONS AS USUAL?

IF YOUR FRIENDS ASKED YOU TO MEET THEM AT THE BEACH FOR A

THE MASS beautifully reveals the relationship between appropriate clothing and interior disposition, between body and soul. The altar is draped in beautiful cloth, and the priest and altar servers wear opulent vestments with richly colored textiles, embroidery, and even lace. The color of the altar cloths and the priest's vestments symbolizes the liturgical season. For example, red is worn on the feast of a martyr, someone who died for the Faith, to symbolize the blood he or she shed for Christ. At a wedding, both the bride and the priest wear white, which points to the purity and newness of marriage.

When we make space for Christ in our body by wearing our Sunday best, we also make space for Him in our soul. We reflect the beauty God has given us, and we make a gift of ourselves to Him. We acknowledge that we are His, "clothed in strength and dignity." Some commentary on this verse from Proverbs suggest that the word "clothed" is a metaphor for the readiness of the woman of worth, and I think this is beautiful to contemplate. Our clothing is a mode of self-expression that readies us for our mission. When you are choosing any outfit, think about what makes you feel strong and dignified. What makes you feel confident, beautiful, and set apart? Wear that!

Rather than make this conversation about whether we ought to wear pants or skirts, let's celebrate our femininity and individuality and use our best judgment. Decide what your unique Sunday best is—likely your personal style amped up a few notches. Go Worthy of Wearing times one hundred for Sundays!

*"She is clothed with strength and dignity,
and laughs at the days to come."*

PROVERBS 31:25

One last point I encourage you to remember about dressing for the contexts we live in, our vocation, and the holy worship of God is that we cannot achieve perfection on earth. We make mistakes; we may try something and discover it does not suit us. That's part of pursuing both holiness and self-expression. Moreover, you may see another woman who, as part of her own path, is trying something new. Maybe she is unaware of the Worthy of Wearing message. I encourage you not to judge her but to befriend her. After becoming her sister in Christ, then you can share with her what you have learned about style and self-worth. By being true friends and living our lives as witnesses of Christ's love, we can gently encourage one another and hand on the truth that we are Worthy of Wearing.

01. What is your vocational season? You may be one or more of the following: a student, a working professional, a missionary, a mother of little ones or teens, a caretaker, or an empty nester. Maybe you're discerning religious life, dating, married, single, or postpartum.

02. What is your local climate like, and how often does it change throughout the year?

03. Is your locality rural, suburban, or urban?

04. What contexts do you frequent every week (in the home, out of the home, community events, events central to your mission)?

05. Which occasions, both formal and informal, do you dress for weekly, monthly, and yearly?

06. What are your weekday "basics"? What do you reach for most often?

07. What items do you think are missing from your wardrobe that would make getting dressed faster?

08. Are you holding on to items from past seasons of your life? Do they fit? Are they future heirlooms? Or could they benefit someone else who may need those very pieces?

FIND
YOUR
SEASON

CHAPTER X

CURATE YOUR WARDROBE LIKE A STYLIST

curate

YOUR

wardrobe

LIKE A

STYLIST

With a trained eye, stylists can look at one stand-alone piece and imagine a whole outfit around it. Having learned from the pros, I have picked up some excellent tips for curating your Worthy Wardrobe. I'm going to teach you exactly what to do! Begin with a blank page and write "MY STYLE" at the top. I want you to have this space to doodle, dream, and write down ideas. You can even start a little inspiration file, whether paper or digital.

An important note as we begin: we reveal our feminine genius, in all its complexity, when we focus on what we like and what works for us. We cannot be boxed into tired style typologies that are so common in women's media. Having to be either the bohemian girl or the preppy girl discourages us from expressing ourselves authentically—yet another example of how the fashion industry often conflicts with style. It's okay to cherry-pick pieces from a range of genres. In fact, the most interesting and memorable outfits harmonize many different eras and trends. Imagine pairing high-waisted, flared jeans from the 1970s with a '50s pastel pink mohair twinset, a vintage '20s brooch, and of-the-moment snake-print slides. This outfit combines styles from four decades—and it works!

When we dress from a mannequin or wear an outfit exactly as shown in the store, our clothes almost always seem to wear us, instead of the other way around. We have to take the nuances of our shape, the contexts we frequent, and all of our unique likes and dislikes into consideration. Anyone can put on a white top and a black bottom, but what makes these garments part of our style is simply how we wear them. Personal style is in the details: how a woman fixes her hair, what perfume she wears, how she grooms her nails, which shoes she prefers, and what jewelry she chooses. Each of these choices reflects her story and identity.

HOW TO CREATE A VISION BOARD TO FIND YOUR WORTHY WARDROBE

Creating a vision board for your style is a worthwhile investment of your time. I like to use digital vision boards, but you can create physical ones as well. Have fun with it! You can use images of outfits other women have put together, collages of your favorite things, or even pieces you already own. You can have a board for each season of the year, for the various contexts you frequent in your daily life, and for colors or patterns you love wearing. I do the same thing with makeup looks I want to recreate!

Include a range of styles from dressed up to dressed down as well as outfits for all kinds of weather. Draw inspiration from designers, photography, fashion, and books on style. Look at sacred art, films, blogs, historical fashions, and local bystanders when you're out and about. You can pull images from websites, magazines, fashion show collections, catalogues, lookbooks, brands, and even nature.

TO START WITH

make three boards: one for daily wear, one for casual or weekend looks, and one for dressed-up styles. Here are some tips to help you get the most out of your vision board:

01.
Include only things you would actually wear, instead of cluttering your vision with items you simply admire.

02.
See if you already have some of the items featured on your board. Even if you don't have the exact pieces, you might have something similar, just in a different color.

03.
Decide whether you can recreate the looks on your board with what you already own. Can you make a few swaps? Should you add any missing items to your to-buy list?

Instead of wishing you could dress like "that girl," take practical steps to achieve the style you are dreaming of. Small tweaks truly make a big difference in your overall aesthetic.

Now that you've identified the themes of your Worthy Wardrobe, you can be clearer and more intentional about what types of styles suit you and your life-style. Feel free to revisit this every so often as your style evolves.

UNCOVER YOUR SIGNATURE AESTHETIC

Would you go to the store to buy ingredients for dinner without looking at the recipe first? No, so why would you shop for your signature style without a goal in mind? Envision what you want your style to look like, and then find inspiration that matches your vision. Your Worthy Wardrobe will develop accordingly.

Style inspiration can come from an era, public figure, film or book character, muse, fashion designer, region, or music genre. Here is a collection of categories that will help you narrow down and define your style. Each aesthetic includes example pieces to get your ideas flowing. This list is by no means complete, but it does cover consistent style themes.

The Worthy of Wearing Pinterest account has visual representations of each of the following categories to help you visualize some iterations of each (visit www.pinterest.com/worthyofwearing). I like to stick with my top three aesthetics to keep it simple, but if I'm honest, I do gravitate to a few more on occasion, depending on the time of year. That's what keeps style fun! My style is a mix of New Yorker, European chic, and Hollywood glam, with a little rock 'n' roll thrown in during fall and some bohemian pieces for the summer. I can't wait for you to uncover your own!

AMERICANA Members Only jackets, baseball caps, aviators, quilted coats, embroidered knits, jean jackets, chambray shirts, flannel, denim on denim, oversized watches, Henleys, moto vests and jackets, utilitarian pockets, safari jackets, cargo pants, camo print, American flag motifs, and suede fringe.

ATHLEISURE/SPORTY sweats, spandex, raglan sleeves, sports jerseys, tees, backpacks, fleece, mock-turtleneck pullovers, university/team sweatshirts, baseball caps, fanny packs, hoodies, vests, seamless leggings, anoraks, windbreakers, tennis skirts, puffer coats, and cross-trainers.

BEACHY ikat kaftans, smocked tank tops, jumpsuits, tie-dye, Bermuda shorts, crocheted tops or dresses, bold prints, rompers, paisley print, palazzo pants, multicolor stripes, straw hats, bird or palm print, rattan bags, leather sandals, scarf headbands, bright colors, and straw box bags.

BOHEMIAN/'70S mixed prints, strappy flats, platform boots, bangles, scoop necks, beaded necklaces, oversized earrings, fringe bags, mohair sweaters, flared denim, sherpa teddy coats, kimonos, bold patterns, crocheted knits, and asymmetrical hems.

CLASSIC/PREPPY riding boots, sweater sleeves as a scarf, ribbon belts, sweater coats, tortoiseshell accessories, canvas totes, gingham, V-neck sweaters, pleated skirts, rugby stripe tops, charm bracelets, signet rings, polo shirts, plaid, toggle buttons, cardigans, khaki trench coats, chinos, fisherman sweaters, ribbed turtlenecks, and schoolboy blazers.

CORPORATE tuxedo shirts, twinsets, argyle, doctor bags, houndstooth, sheath dresses, diamond studs, pantsuits, ribbed turtlenecks, square-toe flats, loafers, black and navy trousers, and power heels.

COUNTRY cowboy or riding boots, cable-knit sweaters, fringe, bandanas, bolo ties, suede, leather, buffalo check, plaid, statement belt buckles, saddlebags, denim shirts, moccasins, wide brim hats, turquoise jewelry, hobo bags, and overalls.

DEMURE lace, ruffles, bows, bolero jackets, tulle, cat-eye sunglasses, Mary Janes, eyelet, fitted bodice dresses, circle skirts, paneled skirts, grosgrain, faux fur, pom-pom details, drop earrings, peplum, turtlenecks, pastels, pearls, ruching, and micro florals.

EUROPEAN CHIC bateau-neck tops, stud earrings, dainty necklaces, berets, striped turtlenecks, wool peacoats, ballet flats, leather watches, bodysuits, white leather sneakers, Oxford shirts, Breton stripes, cigarette trousers, low heels, ankle boots, and dressed-up basics.

GAMINE menswear pleated pants, leather satchels, wool, silk tie scarves, round sunglasses, brogues, turtleneck sweaters, skinny belts, double-breasted blazers, pintucked shirts, tuxedo pants, fedoras, trench coats, cashmere separates, and wool scarves.

HOLLYWOOD GLAM mermaid skirts, jewel tones, midi dresses, jeweled belts, brooches, box clutches, stoles, swing coats, culottes, gold lamé, lace, back seam pantyhose, geometric print, capes, rhinestones, brocade, satin, belted coats, bold lipstick, wide brim hats, sequin dresses, kimonos, wrap dresses, cloche hats, faux fur, accordion pleats, feathers, Peter Pan collars, and velvet.

MINIMALIST   neutrals, crewnecks, straight-leg pants, tailored pants, notched-collar jackets, silk scarves, mini bags, zipper clutches, pendant necklaces, mock-neck tanks, oversized button-downs, flat-front trousers, boxy tops, tunics, peacoats, Mandarin collars, pencil skirts, loafers, and streamlined basics. Often monochromatic from head to toe.

NEW YORKER   riding bold silhouettes, animal print, blazers, chain strap bags, oversized sunglasses, layered outerwear, bracelet watches, flouncy skirts, jumpsuits, tailored separates, textured hoops, fur collars, denim, dolman sleeves, crocodile belts, all black from head to toe, chain necklaces, silk scarves, leather flats, statement jewelry, slingbacks, Chelsea boots, and patent leather.

ROCK 'N' ROLL/PUNK   studded details, leather, clubmaster glasses, contrast stitching, bomber jackets, band tees, crossbody bags, suspenders, Converse Chuck Taylor All Star sneakers, platform or lace-up boots, plaid, buffalo check, mock-neck tops, snakeskin accessories, motorcycle jackets, skinny pants, and distressed or acid-washed denim.

ROMANTIC   ethereal and weightless fabrics, peasant tops, ruffles, sheer sleeves, kimonos, sweater dresses, slip dresses, oversized knits, tulle, floral prints, lace, mules, locket necklaces, tiered maxi dresses, wide-leg pants, curls, shades of cream and white, puff sleeves, beading, and empire-waist dresses.

SOUTHERN BELLE   twinsets, fruit prints, bow details, madras plaid, derby hats, tiered ruffle dresses, cropped pants, gingham, pearls, straw bags, eyelet, bell sleeves, initial jewelry, bolero jackets, sweetheart necklines, cap sleeves, seersucker, midi dresses, kitten heels, peplum tops, and silk blouses.

TRENDY   costume jewelry, name brands, specific styling, statement pieces, and eye-catching, off-the-runway items. Trends are often centered on an It bag, a style of shoe with preferred toe and heel shapes, and a specific color scheme. Each decade has an overarching trend. For instance, the 1980s were all about neon colors, cone heels with pointy toes, and nylon backpacks or patch-work leather crossbody bags. The 2010s may have been the decade of high-waisted denim, Dad sneakers, bushy brows, and contour makeup.

VICTORIAN   embroidery, satin, velvet, stiff collars, floral beading, micro florals, bow ties, drop earrings, chokers, corsets, buttoned cuffs, lace cuffs, bib collars, intricate sleeves, covered buttons, full skirts, lacing, and high lace collars.

The different ways God created us could take pages to list. We were all made in His image, and yet each of us is unique. I love seeing the diversity and intricacy in a woman's features, all handpicked by God — they are worthy of celebrating! Our physical features, including our hair, skin tone, eye color, beauty marks, freckles, height, torso length, and curves are an integral part of our style.

Well-fitting clothes make us feel comfortable and confident, whereas ill-fitting garments are a fast track to feeling insecure and confined. Clothes that are too big or too small can distract us and those around us. Look out for creases across the crotch, lopsided shoulders, bunching across the middle, and dragging hems, and avoid clothing with low-cut armholes, too-short sleeves, and so on. Comfortable clothes don't have to be baggy, and flattering clothes don't have to be second-skin.

Stylists start by taking measurements. These numbers are not meant to upset or deter you. On their own, they have no bearing on your worth, but you can use them to find garments that fit well. You will feel more confident in clothing that beautifully hugs your shape, rather than swallowing or constricting it.

OBTAIN A TAILOR'S MEASURING TAPE, AND MEASURE THE FOLLOWING:

Your BUST. Start at the upper third of your back and measure along the fullest part of your chest.

Your WAIST. Start at the bottom of your rib cage, above your belly button, and relax your tummy.

Your HIPS. Start a few inches down from the crest of your pelvic bone and measure around the widest part of your hips.

Your INSEAM. Start from your inner ankle bone and measure up to the crease of your thigh, called the crotch.

Your ARM LENGTH. Start with your arm bent, with your hand on your hip, and measure from your wrist bone up to your shoulder bone at the top of your arm.

Your SHIRT LENGTH. Start from the side of the base of your neck and measure down to your hip bone. If you want to tuck in your shirt, measure to the crotch marking of your pants.

Now that you know your measurements, shopping online and in person will be much easier. Simple size charts are often on hand to help you find the best fit. Remember that because our bodies change often, as discussed in chapter 9, it's important to repeat these measurements with every new season.

MEASUREMENT RATIOS

Next is your figure. You may have been taught that your figure is a fruit or a geometric shape. Maybe your frame has been called "athletic" or "boyish." It's true that our bodies do come in particular shapes. It's also true that the fashion industry's common yet disappointing classification system for these shapes fails to capture the union of body and soul that we are. As my six-year-old commented, "Women are not apples; they're humans."

Women do not need to dress for their specific body type, because again, style is much more complex than that. For example, a woman with identical measurements for her bust, waist, and hips might love wearing wrap dresses, which is her prerogative, even though most style guidelines would consider wrap dresses a no-no for her body type. However, as I will describe in this section, you can use styling tricks to create symmetry, which will accentuate and enhance your God-given shape. Imagine a horizontal line across your bust, waist, and hips. If you have a wide waist and narrow hips, a boxy jacket that ends at the hips will create a block shape. But a jacket that ends under the rib cage or at the knees will draw the eye to the narrower hip line.

The following recommendations apply even if your measurements fluctuate. Remember, our bodies are meant to change as we carry babies, work, suffer, and age. The size we wear at seventy-seven won't be the one we wore in high school. Similarly, after giving birth, a woman might have an entirely different figure. Rather than trying to "bounce back," let's just keep leaping through the different stages of life with joy and tenacity. If we use our measurements as a guide and follow a few styling tricks, we can feel like ourselves, no matter how our bodies change.

BUST = HIPS > WAIST   If your bust is roughly the same size as your hips, while your waist is narrower, you may find wrap dresses, high-waisted bottoms, tucked-in tops, and cinched belts flattering. Tops with V-necks or scoop necks draw the eye to the waist. Voluminous sleeves can throw off the balance created by a narrow waist and make the bust look wider, so try fitted sleeves (you can play with various sleeve lengths to add variety). Similarly, bulky tops and too-short jackets will widen the waist, so opt for peplum, belted, and fitted styles. Shift dresses hide the cinch under the rib cage, whereas tapered-waist sheaths and wrap dresses look more flattering. Bottoms with a higher rise also highlight the waist by creating a horizontal line at the narrowest part of the midsection. A low-rise bottom, on the other hand, will create a boxy look. Have fun with slim-fit, straight-leg, or flared pants. Trumpet, accordion, and circle skirts will accentuate a narrow waist as well.

BUST = HIPS = WAIST   If your bust is roughly the same size as your hips and waist, you may find that longline sweaters, long poncho wraps, cropped pants, and tea-length skirts create clean lines to outline your shape. Tops that stop at the widest part of your hips and look tight through the bust create too much volume around the waist. The result tends to be a box shape rather than a symmetrical figure eight. Feel free to add volume to the shoulders with a puff sleeve or to the legs with culotte pants. These pieces will add curves. You will also look fabulous in pencil skirts, shift dresses, and column-shaped maxi dresses.

BUST > HIPS = WAIST   If your bust is wider than your hips and waist, create balance for your bottom half by adding volume with a trapeze-style top, which is wider near the hips. High-neck tops make the bust look blocky, while scoop-neck tops show the shape of the neck and create an open space between the fabric and the chin, so the body looks less top-heavy. Boyfriend, boot-cut, pleated, and wide-leg pants will also balance the bottom half by adding width. Pants with a slim or skinny fit will only accentuate your wider bust. The same goes for cropped tops or jackets. Belted jackets, on the other hand, will draw the eye to the waist. Try tiered, A-line, tulip, and box-pleated skirts and dresses that flow and have a pop of color to draw the eye downward.

BUST = HIPS < WAIST   If your bust and hips are smaller than your waist, try wearing scoop- or square-neck tops that are more fitted in the bust and looser in the middle. A-line tunics, trapeze tops, waterfall cardigans, longline sweaters, and blouses that hem below the hips or longer will add balance above and below the waist. Flutter or dolman sleeves that graze the elbow soften a wider bust. Similarly, bolero or similarly structured jackets make the bust look more fitted and the waist more defined. Try mid-rise bottoms, such as A-line skirts that sit above the hip bone and flowy pants without embellishment or pleating. Also consider empire-waist dresses, which wrap beneath the bust and flow downward.

N O W that you can recognize your body's shape, you can find items that will create visual balance, highlight your features, and fit well, creating a polished look. My body has traveled through many of these ratios and proportions as I have become pregnant and given birth three times. My goal is to help you accept that your body will likely change at some point, perhaps more than once, and give you the tools to feel worthy in each new season.

Two other measurements to consider when finding the right items are your height and the length of your torso. Some pieces hang differently depending on the size of a woman's frame. Likewise, the length of a woman's torso may mean she needs to wear a certain dress as a tunic, with slim-cut pants underneath. Taking your proportions into account can make all the difference in your style.

SHORTER TORSO Clothing that accentuates the bust can make a short midsection look even shorter. You can create balance with certain cuts and lengths. A scoop-neck top, for instance, creates an open space near the neck. Hip-grazing jackets (maybe even with peekaboo lace trim) and longline sweaters that end around mid-calf will also elongate your torso. Avoid cropped styles and try wearing your tops untucked. If you do tuck in a top, pull the fabric out about two inches and let it hang over the waist so it looks a bit longer. A pair of high-waisted pants may swallow your waist right up to your bust, whereas a mid-rise or low-rise pair allows more space between your bust and hips. Cropped ankle-length pants, and skirts that end just above the knee will also make your torso look longer and more balanced with a shorter midsection. Long pendant necklaces may fall below your belly button and conflict with the waistband of your bottoms, so try shorter lengths that fall four fingers' length from the bottom of your neck.

LONGER TORSO A longer midsection can make the legs look shorter. Elongate the leg line visually by wearing items such as high-waisted, flared bottoms, high-waisted skirts, and maxi-length empire-waist dresses. High-rise pants draw attention to the length of the inseam, whereas a low-rise pant will make the legs appear even shorter. Tucked-in, fitted tops, cropped jackets that end right above the hip bone, and flowy blouses that float over the waistline add balance to a longer midsection by making the waist appear higher. Belting jackets, tops, and dresses an inch or two higher than your natural waist creates a similar effect. Look for tie-front tops and tops with ruffles, puff sleeves, peplum, or ribbing. These will add detail and volume to the top half and slightly shorten the torso when paired with a high-waisted bottom.

PETITE FRAME Many women with a petite frame can struggle with the inseam length and rise height of pants (the measurement from crotch to belly button), as well as the length of tops and dresses. Knowing your measurements will make shopping for the right sizes much easier. Avoid clothes that swallow your figure from neck to ankles. A few good pairs of tailored pants, skirts above the knee, and comfortable tops you can tuck in will look super polished. Many brands now offer petite sizes, which have shorter sleeves, tops, and dress hems, but they are unlikely to be found in most brick-and-mortar shops. Online shopping may be your best bet. To get the best fit possible, find a reputable dry cleaner-tailor who can make small, inexpensive adjustments, including removing excess fabric. Your clothing will look custom-made without the big price tag.

TALL FRAME Women with a tall frame may have difficulty finding tops that hem at the hip and pants that end at the ankle bone instead of the mid-calf. In addition, depending on your body, clothing labeled high-rise could fall as mid-rise. To find the right fit for you, note the actual length of the garment's rise and compare it to the distance between your crotch and your belly button. Straight-leg and skinny pants and A-line skirts are super flattering on a tall frame, as are maxi dresses with a defined waist. Have some fun with jumpsuits, which are often cut longer, and experiment with different belts and necklaces to play with proportion. Large, boxy cuts might look too overwhelming on a tall frame, so look for pieces that fall neatly over your shoulders and curves, naturally highlighting your figure.

CLOTHING CATEGORIES

Let's get familiar with a few terms that will help you differentiate what types of clothing you need to fulfill your mission and feel confident while doing so. Your clothing falls into three basic categories: foundations, workhorses, and jaw-droppers.

FOUNDATIONS are the basics that form the first layer of every outfit. Underwear, socks, T-shirts, pajamas, slips, and camisoles fall under this category, as do simple sundresses and jeans. Like a crumb coating on a cake, they create a smooth foundation for the next layer. Foundations are the first pieces you'll put on every day. Usually, they are made from breathable, easily laundered fabrics and need to be replaced regularly because they are washed and worn so often. Don't feel obligated to spend a lot on foundations. Just look for items made of natural fibers, such as cotton and linen, as these will hold up well to daily wear. (For example, my foundations include simple slip dresses, white or black T-shirts and crewneck tanks, white button-downs, and high-waisted jeans.) What are your foundations?

WORKHORSES are the items that you can wear over your base layer to instantly add style and polish. Examples include jackets, blazers, sweaters, coats, quality shoes, belts, sturdy handbags, figure-enhancing dresses or skirts, tailored pants, and reliable blouses. These items are the layer of frosting applied on top of the crumb coating to finish off the cake. Workhorses are essential — they tie an outfit together, create a coherent look, and make up your signature style. (For example, my workhorses include velvet or wool blazers, leather shoes, a motorcycle jacket, belts with a chunky buckle, shirtdresses, flat-front trousers, and a black leather tote.) What are your workhorses?

JAW-DROPPERS make a statement and add pep in your step. Think of them as the powdered sugar dusting on the cake. Too little sugar makes the cake bland, while too much takes away from its flavor. You probably own a few jaw-droppers already, but maybe you don't wear them as often as you should. Celebrate each day you're given with a little something extra from this category. It's easy to include a jaw-dropping accessory (even an on-trend one) without making a huge commitment. A sparkly cocktail ring, geometric earrings, a bold bangle, a silky printed scarf, a brightly colored dress, a printed skirt, a beaded bag, colorful eyeglasses, or a punchy maxi coat can be just that little bit extra your outfit needs to showcase your personality in a playful way. (For example, my jaw-droppers include a leopard-print scarf, cat-eye sunglasses, a rust-colored trench coat, a velvet shoe, a bone-colored suede motorcycle vest, a Figaro chain bracelet, a gold watch, and bright red beaded earrings.) What are your jaw-droppers? Do they suit your state in life?

CLOTHING SILHOUETTES

Read through these clothing silhouettes to become familiar with how garments are described. These descriptions, although not exhaustive, will help you research styles you love for your vision board, and will assist you as you shop for items on your to-buy list. To help you visualize your Worthy Wardrobe, check out the Worthy of Wearing Pinterest account (**www.pinterest.com/worthyofwearing**), where you'll find examples of the following silhouettes. Look through the items you already love in your closet and see what necklines, waistlines, and styles you feel worthy of wearing.

NECKLINES boatneck (a bateau), cowl neck, scoop neck, keyhole, funnel, turtleneck, V-neck, crewneck, square neck, sweetheart neck, halter.

SLEEVE STYLES sleeveless, three-quarter sleeve, short sleeve, long sleeve, cap sleeve, dolman sleeve.

SHIRT STYLES western, pintucked, tuxedo, ruffle-front, peasant, blouse, tunic, Henley, polo, T-shirt.

PANT STYLES wide leg, flared, boot cut, palazzo, button fly, cargo, sailor, pleated, slim fit, boyfriend fit, cropped, tapered leg, harem.

DRESS STYLES sheath, wiggle, bodycon, tent, tunic, apron, slip, baby doll, peasant, shirt-dress, wrap, blouson, halter, strapless.

SKIRT STYLES trumpet, box-pleated, mini, accordion, tiered, sarong, fit-and-flare, mermaid, tulip, A-line, circle, pencil, panel, maxi, midi (tea length), wrap, straight.

WAISTLINES empire, drawstring, pointed, bandless, banded, paper bag, shirred, drop waist, peplum, pintucked, high-waisted, hip-hugger (low rise).

COLOR PALETTES

A COLOR PALETTE might sound artsy, but the idea here is to identify which colors you love wearing *the most*. Pick eight favorite colors and see how they go together. It helps to have a few neutrals in hues that suit your eyes, skin tone, and hair. The neutrals in my color palette are black, white, rust, denim blue, blood red, olive green, camel, and navy. Try to wear no more than two or three colors in one outfit, even when you're mixing prints or color blocking. That way, your outfit doesn't look costumey, but effortlessly chic.

Once you've identified your top eight shades, you'll have a much easier time shopping for clothes and getting dressed. If you'd like to dig deeper into color swatching or simply find out which colors complement each other, you can find lots of resources online.

NEUTRALS Usually, neutrals consist of earth tones, such as chocolate brown, olive green, brick red, cream, navy, ecru, taupe, camel, rust, stone gray, and black. Animal prints are also considered neutrals, since animals live in nature.

MONOCHROMATIC Choose any color under the sun and wear it from head to toe! It's easy if your pieces match, and it looks cohesive and effortless.

COLOR BLOCKING Pair two colors, one on top and one on bottom, to create an eye-catching contrast. Try combining black and white, cherry red and fuchsia, pale blue and emerald green, navy and pale pink, or camel and violet!

PATTERN MIXING Combine two patterns, such as florals and stripes, polka dots and geometric prints, plaid and leopard print, or small florals and big florals. The key is to make sure the shades overlap. Do the patterns contain similar colors? Do they have the same background color? A black-and-white striped top could look incredible with a black-and-white houndstooth jacket or skirt. The result is playful but still polished.

TIMELESS PIECES THAT LAST

Classic, always chic, and mostly practical, these pieces easily create a timeless capsule within your wardrobe for any decade. Invest in items made of high-quality natural fibers, such as cotton and wool, and look for neutral colors and traditional silhouettes. You will have these pieces forever, and you can keep them updated by adding modern accessories.

TOPS button-down Oxford shirts, blouses, blazers, trench coats, peacoats, cardigans, crew-neck sweaters, and white T-shirts.

DRESSES dark (navy, chocolate brown, heather gray, or black) knee-length or midi dresses, white sundresses, and printed long-sleeve dresses.

LOUNGEWEAR matching sets of knitwear or sweatpants, duster sweaters, leggings, Pima cotton tops.

BOTTOMS circle skirts, pencil skirts, straight-leg jeans, chinos, and black or navy trousers.

SHOES plain white lace-up sneakers, black heels, tan leather sandals, cognac boots, and rubber rain boots.

The current season and the climate where we live often dictate which fabrics we find most comfortable. If you've ever worn linen in the winter, you know how little warmth it retains — making it more appropriate for summer. Here's a starting point for keeping your Worthy Wardrobe updated throughout the year.

COLD WEATHER FABRICS velvet, corduroy, gabardine, wool, cashmere, faux fur, suede, patent leather, fleece, chenille, leather, satin, tweed, flannel, yarn, sequins, lamé, velour, felt, jacquard, mohair, and sherpa.

WARM WEATHER FABRICS linen, chambray, seersucker, silk, canvas, gingham, jersey, viscose, eyelet, mesh, terrycloth, madras, crochet, and ikat.

FABRICS FOR ALL YEAR ROUND silk, cotton, crêpe, lace, spandex, denim, tulle, poplin, chiffon, organza, dotted swiss, and French terry.

FABRIC BLENDS viscose, rayon, and polyester are all synthetic fabrics worn year-round. Remember, synthetics are usually better in colder weather because they retain heat and do not breathe as well as cotton, linen, and silk. These fabrics are often fickle with how long they last before looking worn, but they usually cost less. They also require careful laundering. You may need to wash pieces made of these fabrics in cold water and then hang them to dry. Keep this in mind when you shop, and always check the inside tag for details.

ACCESSORIZE LIKE A PRO

Accessories are the key to personalizing anything you wear. They make the little details of your story, your mission, and your personality shine through. You can transform a garment on a hanger into a part of who you are simply by adding your favorite accessories. Try on a rhinestone bracelet, tie a silk scarf around your neck, or throw on some brightly colored shoes. See which items from the list below jump out at you and add them to your vision board. If you're missing a few, update your to-buy list.

Remember, less is more. French designer Coco Chanel famously said, "Before you leave the house, look in the mirror and take one thing off." A chunky necklace worn with a printed top, long earrings, bright lipstick, a floppy hat, colored tights, and statement shoes is visually overwhelming. If you stick to wearing two or three colors max and avoid going overboard on accessories, your style will always look effortless, and your confidence will rise.

BELTS grommet, wide, skinny, woven, fabric, O-ring, rope, leather-backed ribbon, braided, crocodile, suede, corset, western, double buckle, studded, animal print, chain.

BRACELETS bangle, friendship, leather, charm, pearl, chain, beaded, cuff.

BROOCHES jeweled, metal, cloth, floral, feathered.

EARRINGS chandelier, stud, hoop, dangle, teardrop, leverback, drop, J-hoop, cuff, shoulder-duster.

GLASSES aviator, cat-eye, round, oval, square, wayfarer, clubmaster, wrap, readers.

GLOVES lace, leather, suede, fingerless, knit, mittens, long-sleeve.

HAIR CLIPS claw, snap, banana, barrette.

HANDBAGS hobo, crossbody, satchel, bucket, tote, clutch.

HATS western, pillbox, straw, visor, floppy wide brim, baseball cap, beret, fedora.

HEADBANDS turban, hatband, wide, thin, knotted, sporty elastic.

NECKLACES choker, bib, lariat, chain, collar, long and short pendants, statement.

RINGS cocktail, band, solitaire, Claddagh, birthstone, signet, engagement, stacked, class rings.

SCARVES handkerchief, blanket, poncho, pashmina, knit, rectangle, shawl, infinity, neckerchief.

SHOES

   MATERIALS pony hair, rubber, suede, leather, patent leather, cork, acrylic, faux leather, faux suede, faux patent leather, denim, beads, studs, rhinestones, glitter.

   FRONT OF THE SHOE almond toe, pointy toe, round toe, square toe, open toe, peep toe, T-strap, ankle strap, monk strap, ballet, loafer, brogue, Mary Jane.

   HEEL OF THE SHOE block heel, stiletto, kitten heel, wedge, covered wedge, cone heel, court heel, platform, flatform, d'Orsay, sling back, mule, clog, flat, espadrille.

   BOOTS combat, Chelsea, riding, ankle, go-go, platform, western, over-the-knee, hiking, Ugg.

   SANDALS gladiator, strappy, flip-flops, Tevas, slides.

TIGHTS opaque, sheer, fishnet, knit, lace, logo.

BEAUTY IS AN ACCESSORY

Just as we can use clothing and accessories for self-expression and adornment, so we can personalize our style with how we wear makeup, style our hair, and care for our nails. The beauty category of personal style is one more way to let your identity shine. The simplest outfit (such as a white sundress) can look sportier, dressier, or more casual depending on the shoes, makeup, and hairstyle you pair it with.

White sundress + ponytail + sneakers + diamond studs + lip balm = SPORTY

White sundress + hair down in beachy waves + beaded gladiator sandals + gold hoops + berry lipstick = DRESSY

White sundress + hair in low bun + flip-flops + lip gloss = CASUAL

A signature skin regimen and makeup routine is just one more way to refine your personal style and make it truly reflect who you are. Maybe you prefer not to wear makeup, relying only on high-quality skincare products. Maybe you like to use a little concealer to brighten and even your complexion, pencil or gel to define your brows, and mascara to create contrast with your pupils, making the whites of your eyes even brighter. Or maybe you're a little like me, and you feel ready for the day with foundation, cream blush, some shimmering eyeshadow, a dusting of bronzer, mascara, brow gel, and lipstick.

No matter where you fall on the spectrum, paying attention to your skin is important. Our face is sacred. It allows us to show emotion and communicate with others. With smiles, expressive eyebrows, rosy cheeks, laugh lines, and beauty marks, we use our femininity to nurture another person, to make him or her feel seen and loved. When we care for our skin, our complexion glows. We invite others to greet us, and so much good can come from that invitation.

A simple daily skincare routine will make all the difference in helping your skin age gracefully and creating a hydrated canvas that makes wearing makeup look even more natural and less noticeable. If you are looking to create a daily skincare regimen that takes sixty seconds or less, start with a cleanser that will retain the moisture barrier of the skin without stripping it, and remove makeup, bacteria, and environmental toxins. Look for a cleanser that matches your skin type (most women have either dry, dry-combination, oily-combination, or oily skin).

SKINCARE, STEP BY STEP:

———————

(WITH SUN PROTECTION IF YOU PLAN TO BE OUTSIDE)

CLEANSER; TREATMENT SUCH AS A SERUM, TONER,

MINERAL ESSENCE, OR MIST; MOISTURIZER

MAKEUP CHECKLIST:

If you need a simple makeup routine to get started, I like to recommend one complexion product to even the skin and reduce any redness or discoloration. That could be a concealer, foundation, or tinted moisturizer. Next is something to groom the brows and brush them upward to create openness around the eyes. Brow gel, a brow pencil, eyeshadow, or even just a stiff spoolie brush can define and frame your face, directing another person's gaze to yours. Then, add warmth or brightness to your cheeks with bronzer or blush. It's amazing how playing with light and shadow can make us look well rested and add dimension to our skin. For lips, you can add a little balm, gloss, or lipstick. Draw attention to your smile with some color or shine! Add a little mascara to curled lashes to create openness around your beautiful eyes, and that's it.

If you want your makeup to look as natural as possible, start by caring for your skin, purchasing high-quality products with safe ingredients, and using shades that enhance your skin tone, eye color, and hair color. You're a natural beauty!

Now that you are armed with a vision for your style, you can define it and begin to build a cohesive wardrobe around it. If you still have some lingering confusion, try going through the Worthy of Wearing style boards on Pinterest by process of elimination. Once you have determined what is not you, your true style will reveal itself. Match that with your state in life, and season of life, and you will be unstoppable! The vision is what takes the most time to develop, but with time and patience, you will start to notice patterns in what attracts you, what makes you feel most confident, and what truly suits you — whether you are shopping for an evening gown, a bathing suit, or loungewear.

CHAPTER XI

SHOP
WITH
INTENTION

SHOP

with

INTENTION

Shopping for new clothing can be overwhelming. Big-box stores are often overstocked, thrifting is time-consuming and takes a keen eye, and online shopping is intimidating, since you have no way to feel the garment before buying. On top of all, you have to determine how much money you can allocate to creating a Worthy Wardrobe.

Part of shopping with intention, especially on a small budget, is knowing how to use the pieces you already have. The famous actress Audrey Hepburn, who starred in iconic movies such as *Funny Face, Roman Holiday, Charade,* and *Breakfast at Tiffany's* — some of my personal favorites — is an excellent example of someone who created a memorable style using very little. According to the children's book *Just Being Audrey* by Margaret Cardillo: "Audrey had only a few blouses and skirts and one colorful scarf. But she could tie the scarf twenty different ways to make a new outfit every day."[12] Audrey Hepburn's childhood and adolescence took place during World War II, when resources were scarce. People learned to take great care of their belongings and used them as long as possible. Clothing was mended when it ripped, not thrown right in the trash. Old garments were often cut into scraps to create something entirely new.

Owning a simplified wardrobe forces us to be creative (and grateful) for what we have. And in wearing the same types of clothes in a cohesive color palette or range of prints that we feel great in, we create a signature style. Audrey Hepburn's style wasn't admired because of its variety but because of its cohesiveness and authenticity. Think of a few women whose style you admire. I'm sure certain descriptions or iconic pieces come to mind immediately!

Another children's book we can look to and share with our families that depicts the importance of being creative with our closet is Simms Taback's *Joseph Had a Little Overcoat*, which won the Caldecott Medal in 2000. Joseph started with an overcoat, and as the years went on, it became a jacket, a vest, a scarf, a necktie, and finally a button. The sweet story shows the different occasions Joseph attended with his ever-changing garment. He made the effort to look dignified, even with a deteriorating overcoat.

Like Joseph and Audrey, when I was a child, I had to develop a sense of style with the "leftover" garments I had: hand-me-downs, clearance-rack items, secondhand store finds, and clothing from outlet brands. I didn't often wear something completely new with a shiny brand label, and when I did, it was usually a birthday gift. My love of personal expression through clothing and styling developed largely from the desperation of wanting what was trendy and having a limited selection to choose from. My peers all wore brand names, and I wanted my secondhand style to look brand new. What I discovered was that sticking to neutral colors and simpler shapes made my clothing look "in" every season, even if it was still the same black turtleneck I bought last fall. I also found that dark-colored clothing tends to look more "expensive" and classy, even if it didn't cost much at all. Cheaply made garments don't have the tight seams, heavy buttons, or incredible fabrics and dyes of most high-end garments, but if you use these little

tips, you can look like you shop at a luxury store without having to pay luxury prices.

One of my favorite co-workers at Saks Fifth Avenue was a woman in her sixties who loved to shop designer brands. Like most of us makeup artists, she wore a lot of black, and her chunky silver accessories and Chanel sunglasses always made her look magnetic. She was one of those women who immediately made you want to know her!

Even her trained eye couldn't detect my bargain finds. When she would tell me, "Oh, I love those pants. Where did you find them?" I used to crack her up by replying that they were from a store at the mall.

What I learned from my childhood experience, and from years of working in retail and fashion, is that you do not need a hefty bank balance to have genuine, attractive personal style. In fact, my co-workers who had the means to own anything they desired often suffered with decision paralysis as a result. No matter the size of your clothing budget, truly knowing yourself and your mission is vital to expressing externally what already exists in your soul.

PLAN A CLOTHING BUDGET

The worst thing we can do for our clothing budget, not to mention our hope of having a cohesive wardrobe, is shopping without a plan. Many of us, including me, have shopped unnecessarily out of boredom or curiosity. Before you shop, inventory your closet with the Edit, which I have laid out for you in the next few pages. You should also create a plan for exactly how much you can spend. (If you plan a family budget, include a line for each member of your family.) Remember, clothing is a non-negotiable category of your budget! We need clothing in order to accomplish our specific daily tasks and achieve the greatness we are working toward.

When you create a yearly, quarterly, or monthly shopping budget, you eliminate the guilty feeling that creeps in when your trip to the wholesale store for pantry staples includes purchasing a jacket that caught your eye. If you had a jacket on your to-buy list, your purchase fills a need, and there is no need to feel guilty. Win-win!

SMALL BUDGET TIPS:

1. Take good care of your clothing, and you can easily resell it or trade it at a clothing swap with friends! Air dry your clothes when possible and learn how to mend buttons and tears. But don't stop there: look for things around the house that could be sold. Put that money toward your budget for new pieces. Even an extra twenty dollars can go a long way at a secondhand store.

2. Decide how much you can spend annually, and then break that amount down by month. For some of us, shopping more frequently for smaller purchases is a little easier than spending large sums all at once. And this way, you can keep up with changing seasons and new needs that may arise.

Prudence, shopping, and intentionality can go together. These tips will help you curate a complete wardrobe and shop smarter. When you have a wardrobe that is edited down to items that both bring you joy and express your uniqueness in Christ, your self-confidence will be contagious! Getting dressed each morning will be much more efficient, allowing you to get on with your day.

THE EDIT

The first place we'll shop is our closet! Let's begin the Edit: a process for creating a Worthy Wardrobe. We're going to clear out the clutter and slim down our options to make sure every piece we own makes us feel confident, joyful, and ready for the day.

Set aside one hour to edit your closet. You'll need three paper grocery bags, a Sharpie, and — to give your space a cozy feel — your favorite drink, candles, and a playlist, podcast, or audiobook. Have a mirror close by for try-ons. Now, mark the grocery bags: "donate," "resell," and "recycle."

Give yourself permission to let go of what is cluttering your closet and confusing your style. I know just how difficult it can be to part with gifts, clothes that hold many memories, or items that you hoped would fit better someday. For years, I held on to a coat my dad got me, because it was expensive and it made me think of him. But the coat just didn't suit me, and it was taking up valuable real estate in my closet. Finally, I chose to pass it on to a friend. To my surprise, it brought her so much joy. She said it was a coat she'd always dreamed of owning!

Giving my coat away created space in my wardrobe, physically and mentally, and made my friend's day. When we choose to create space for items that make us feel special, we can more peacefully pass on the items we no longer need. We can still hold on to our memories and feelings of love and appreciation for the gifts and their givers. In turn, we can let go of the feelings of disappointment and shame that arise when we come across those ill-fitting items, whose presence seems to belittle us. Rest assured that they will go to a new home and bring someone else joy.

Cut your closet down to what you feel *worthy* in. You are the editor in chief of your wardrobe, and what you wear matters. Remember, you are dressing your *current* life, your *current* body, and your *current* mission. Your clothing has to work for you, and everything else is unnecessary. Simplicity is key. Plus, your morning routine is about to get much faster! The most efficient way to get ready every day is to have a wardrobe that you feel worthy of wearing. The goal of the Edit is for you to open your closet each morning to outfits that make you feel truly beautiful and uniquely yourself.

Start the Edit with a simple prayer: "Come, Holy Spirit!"

01. Set aside your most prized pieces — the ones you feel incredible in (and that fit like a glove)! Make a separate place for them in your closet, and section them off for now.

02. Separate your clothes by category. You can put them on your bed, in your closet, or on the floor, whichever works for you. Try on every top, every pair of pants, every skirt, and every sweater. I like to start with dresses, then move on to tops, bottoms, sweaters, jackets, and outerwear. Put away the items that fit, and place the rest in the donate, resell, and recycle bags.

03. If a piece doesn't fit or suit you, or is simply worn out, place it in the appropriate grocery bag. Place the bags out of sight, and if you don't reach for them over the next thirty days, pass them on. Donate to a thrift store, resell through consignment (you can even do this online), or recycle your textiles if possible.

04. Write down which items need to be replaced and which key pieces you need to complete your closet — for instance, a smart jacket, a neutral cardigan, an occasion dress, camisoles, a brown belt, leather sneakers, or tailored pants. This is the beginning of your to-buy list. Your list can be digital or on paper, as long as it's handy when you're out and about. I like to store mine in my phone and check things off as soon as I find them. When inspiration hits, I jot down a few things to remember for the next time I'm out. I add a few new things to my wardrobe about every four to six months to keep things fresh and modern, but I always stick to what suits me and the pieces I already own. Your to-buy list will keep you from getting swept up in what's currently standing out on the racks. It will help you stay laser focused, save money for the things you truly need, and maintain a streamlined personal style that is 100 percent true to you.

When it is time to shop for new items, consider a few things.

01. Is it love at first sight? Does it give you butterflies in your stomach? How excited or joyful do you feel when it catches your eye? Go with your gut feeling. Even foundations — the simple basics — should be so comfortable and well fitting that you look forward to wearing them.

02. Quality: How does the garment need to be laundered? Will it last more than a few washes? Check the tag for synthetic fabrics that pill easily, such as polyester and rayon. Tug on zippers and buttons to see how sturdy they are. This is where your stylist training from chapter 10 comes in.

03. Take note: Is the item you're about to buy the best thing on the rack, or the best thing for your wardrobe? It might be the most attractive item in the store but the worst item in your closet. Even a $6.99 piece is best left at the store if it's just not your style. Save the money for another day (or for coffee with a friend)! Try to avoid items that don't mesh well with the rest of your clothes. They will end up just sitting in the back of your closet.

04. When I am unsure about a piece, I like to walk around the store with it as if I intend to buy it. If I am "over it" by the time I'm ready to check out, the item gets returned to the rack. No harm done!

05. How does it fit? Is it so loose as to swallow your shape? Is it too tight, creasing and pinching at your body? Is the fabric itchy or too sheer? Would you have to buy a very specific undergarment just for this item, and would it be worth it? The size and the name on the tag should never make or break your purchase. Remember, fit trumps size, and quality trumps name brand.

06. How does this item jive with what you already own? Is it a foundation, a workhorse, or a jaw-dropper? If it's just "nice" and doesn't fill a need, leave it! Remember, you're rebuilding your Worthy Wardrobe now that you've completed the Edit. Stick to replacing foundations, investing in workhorses, and sprinkling in jaw-droppers.

07. Take each item for a test drive so you can see how it moves. How easily can you sit, stand, bend, jump, or chase a taxi or a toddler without ripping a seam or exposing yourself? With shoes, ask yourself whether they're "cab to curb" only or comfortable enough for a full day of wear.

08. Replace the most necessary items first. A gorgeous pair of heels might be calling you from across the store, but if what you truly need is a replacement for your tattered tote bag, keep hunting for the right bag and save the shoes for another day.

While shopping, we can easily fall into a scarcity mindset, which leads us to believe that we will never find the same item twice. But that's not the case. Passing up something that looks fun but doesn't fill a need in our wardrobe isn't just okay — it's an opportunity to grow in detachment. I truly believe that when we are prudent, practical, and intentional, even the tiniest blessings will fall upon us as we do ordinary things, including shopping for clothes.

Thrifting is modern-day treasure hunting. There is nothing more exciting than spotting a 100 percent pure silk top that fits like a dream, or a tweed men's blazer that looks as if it came right out of a Sherlock Holmes story. The Brooklyn Flea open-air market in New York is one of my favorite places to find old gems, such as a mint-condition 1960s vintage fur stole. Back when I lived on East 90th Street on the Upper East Side, my best friend and I started countless Saturday mornings thrifting at Housing Works on the corner of 2nd Avenue. We were two fashion girls with champagne taste on a beer budget. After eating breakfast at our favorite local diner, we'd work our way down 2nd Avenue to Goodwill and the Salvation Army, stopping for coffee and snacks in between. Divide and conquer was often our method, so we would start on opposite ends of the same rack and meet in the middle, calling out to each other if we found something worth looking at. With a laugh, we'd hold up a garment and ask, "Why don't I hate this?" Hidden in those racks of outdated, worn-out clothes were vintage and designer pieces that fit as if they'd been custom-made.

Here are a few of my top tips for scoring at the thrift store:

01.   Bring a slip or a thin camisole and seamless underwear to make try-ons even easier. Wear shoes that slide on and off so you don't have to keep tying and buckling.

02.   Look through the racks by the sleeves to save time on browsing. If the sleeve looks well made and in good condition, then open the rack to see the rest of the item.

03.   Go by fit instead of size. Vintage pieces often don't have marked sizes, and those that do don't match current size charts. Hold things up to your body and know your measurements. Use the dressing room when possible.

04.   Look for high-quality fabrics made of natural fibers such as wool, cotton, and silk. One trip to the dry cleaners, or a run-through with a handheld steamer, will make them look as good as new!

Ethics
AND SHOPPING

"Ethical fashion" is a buzzword that has emerged largely in response to so-called fast fashion, or the instantaneous production of mass-market clothing that is less expensive and of lower quality than, say, a custom suit. For decades, the fashion industry traditionally had two seasons of new ready-to-wear styles every year, represented in runway shows. Autumn/winter always shows in February, and spring/summer always shows in September. Over the last fifteen years or so, brands have begun monthly, and sometimes even weekly, drops of new items. This creates buzz and scarcity at the same time, making it impossible not to fall into the machine of trend-chasing.

Often, the production of fast fashion involves problems that the consumer never hears about, such as poor labor conditions, shady sourcing, and worse. Many consumers have begun demanding increased transparency from brands and designers about the laborers sewing the garments, their working conditions, their compensation, and how the textiles are sourced. As a result, "ethical" fashion brands have emerged to combat the throwaway culture created by the widespread demand for instant gratification. These brands work to reduce the massive waste that results from overproduction, and make garments with higher standards, among other things. The simplicity of having fewer, higher-quality items made in dignified conditions is a relief for many consumers.

In a perfect world, we would all buy ethically — but the loosely defined "ethical" label could use some qualifiers. Truth be told, how the clothing industry currently operates makes transparency very difficult. Many brands make donations to corporations and nonprofits that do not uphold Christian values, but much of this activity is still being brought into the light. Until we consumers voice our concerns, things will remain as they are: murky at best. We should aim to be conscious customers while remaining prudent and practical within our means. Not everyone can afford an ethically made garment over one from a box store, but we can all be intentional about our shopping habits and the way we care for our goods. Always be practical: decide what you need, and then find the simplest way to fulfill that need.

I hope shopping for your Worthy Wardrobe feels a little less intimidating now that you have a starting place. Over time, you will perfect your eye and your style so you can find what really works for you and makes who you are shine.

Choose a *patron saint* to help you on your shopping trip! St. Rose of Lima is the patron of beauty. St. Homobonus is the patron of clothworkers, shoemakers, and tailors. St. Veronica is the patron of laundry workers. St. Clare of Assisi is the patron saint of embroidery. St. Barbara is the patron of milliners. St. Anne is the patron of seamstresses.

CHAPTER XII

EMBRACE YOUR JOURNEY

embrace

YOUR

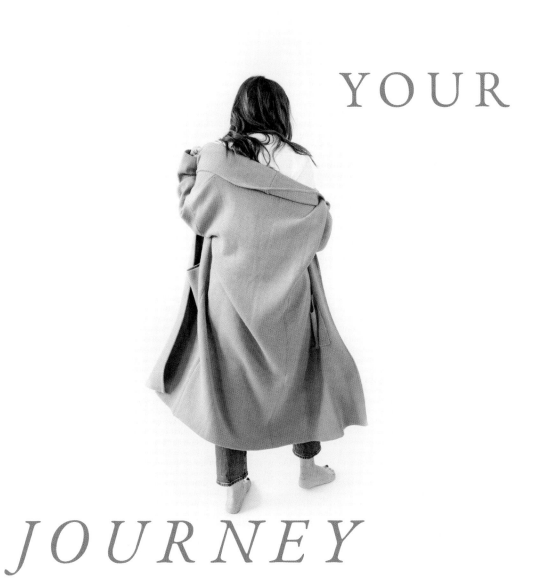

JOURNEY

LIKE FAITH AND HOLINESS, style doesn't come to us all at once over a single month or even a single decade. It's a journey, and we must be aware of and honor where we are on that path, whether we're a novice, an expert, or somewhere in between. Please do not pressure yourself to reach style perfection by the end of this book. Style takes many years to cultivate (and accumulate), so rather than tossing everything and starting from scratch, use your best judgment and be intentional.

Additionally, as life and circumstances change, so does our style — and so does our relationship with God. In some seasons, we may feel closer to God and hear His voice speaking truth to us more often. In other seasons, we may experience a dark night of the soul, during which we feel distant from God and confused about what to do next. This is important to keep in mind when it comes to both your prayer life and your self-image.

Personal style is unique for each person and is really just a genuine expression of the self through clothing. Some of us are more inclined to have a more festive, playful style, while others are grounded in simple shapes and practical fabrics. One woman's style is not decidedly better than another, even though the fashion industry would beg to differ. Personal style is unique to a woman's lifestyle and vocation, so long as she is expressing them authentically. We should celebrate the style of our sisters in Christ, not fall into critiquingwhether it is super "in" right now. Remember, our worth does not come from a closet of new clothes, but from God. Our inherent dignity and our rootedness in Christ's unconditional love give meaning to our clothing, which echoes our interior disposition.

Embracing the Worthy of Wearing mindset means gradually changing our habits. If you commit to taking care of your body and soul every day, and even plan your schedule accordingly, what now feels unusual or special will become a regular part of your routine.

In his book *Furrow*, St. Josemaría Escrivá teaches: "*Nunc coepi!* — Now I begin! This is the cry of a soul in love which, at every moment, whether it has been faithful or lacking in generosity, renews its desire to serve — to love! — our God with a wholehearted loyalty."[13] Jesus Christ conquered death for us, and because of His victory, we can begin again many times over with His grace (and in a special way through the Sacrament of Reconciliation). Do not fall prey to discouragement. Just remember "Nunc coepi"! And say aloud, "Now I begin!" as often as you need.

Giving up on yourself is not an option. Thoughts of fear, confusion, shame, and discouragement do not come from God. His yoke is easy, and His burden is light. Seize each day with hope, and ask for God's graces upon you and your mission. Invite Jesus into the parts of your story that are painful. Invite Jesus into your present mess. Invite Jesus to guide your future with His steady hand.

THIRTY-DAY ACTION PLAN

The Worthy of Wearing mindset takes practice. That's why I have created this thirty-day action plan, which is for every woman, no matter where she is on her style journey. This plan was designed to start any Sunday, with day 1 dedicated to inviting Christ into this process with journaling and prayer time on the Sabbath. Each day has one prompt to help you get out of your comfort zone, uncover your personal style, and develop a wardrobe that reflects who you are. Creating habits around the Worthy of Wearing mindset with your Worthy Wardrobe starts here.

KEY

The thirty days of the #worthyofwearing challenge fall into four categories:

01. **Style Vision (SV):** Create a vision for your style, no matter what season of life you're in.

02. **Try Something New (TSN):** There's no time like the present to shake things up.

03. **Wear Now (WN):** Embrace what you already have and wear it with confidence.

04. **Wardrobe Clean-Out (WCO):** Say goodbye to clutter and edit your wardrobe to a tee.

SUNDAY, DAY 1 SV
Spend time praying and journaling. Ask the Holy Spirit to inspire you, remind you who you are, and help you embrace His vision for you.

MONDAY, DAY 2 TSN
Try a statement earring. (Clip-ons work too!)

TUESDAY, DAY 3 WN
Wear the outfit that makes you feel 100 percent confident.

WEDNESDAY, DAY 4 TSN
Wear a signature bracelet for the rest of the week.

THURSDAY, DAY 5 WN
Wear your favorite shoes and put together an outfit to complement them.

FRIDAY, DAY 6 SV
Identify your basics and write down the categories that each item belongs to. You can separate them into weekday and weekend outfits.

SATURDAY, DAY 7 WCO
Bag up your stained, ripped, misshapen, pilled, faded, or threadbare clothing (including socks and underwear).

SUNDAY, DAY 8 SV
Create your digital inspiration board. You can either copy and paste images onto a blank space or organize them into themes and boards with a free app, such as Pinterest or Evernote.

MONDAY, DAY 9 WN
Wear your favorite necklace. Highlight it with the neckline or color of your top.

TUESDAY, DAY 10 SV
Write down five colors you love to wear in any season. Bonus: find outfits you'd wear in those shades and save them to your vision board.

WEDNESDAY, DAY 11 SV
Choose five words that describe your style.

THURSDAY, DAY 12 WN
Wear your favorite bottom.

FRIDAY, DAY 13 SV
Create your digital to-buy list with the items your closet is missing, so you can make your outfits more complete. Separate the items on your list by category, season, and context (for instance, Sunday best, workwear, weekend outfits, and so on).

SATURDAY, DAY 14 WCO
Try on your remaining clothes after last Saturday's WCO. Separate whatever doesn't fit into bags — one for donations, one for resale, and one for swapping with friends.

SUNDAY, DAY 15 SV
Mass outfits. Try on three to four options that work for church on Sunday. It helps to prepare ahead of time so your Sunday can be less stressful.

MONDAY, DAY 16 SV
Decide on your signature skincare and makeup routine and plan time each day (five to ten minutes in the morning and at night) to care for your skin.

TUESDAY, DAY 17 TSN
Wear a hair accessory of your choice. It could be anything — a pin, a clip, a scarf, or a hat.

WEDNESDAY, DAY 18 SV
Journal about your favorite pieces of clothing and your memories of wearing them. How did you feel when you wore them?

THURSDAY, DAY 19 TSN
Wear the same pattern or color from head to toe.

FRIDAY, DAY 20 WN

Take something casual, such as a white T-shirt or a simple dress, and dress it up with accessories, a fun jacket, or colorful shoes.

SATURDAY, DAY 21 WCO

Go through your accessories (scarves, belts, bags, jewelry, pins, hats, gloves) and shoes. Bag up anything that's worn out or doesn't suit you anymore, or that you don't really love, and put it aside.

SUNDAY, DAY 22 SV

Take a few moments to decide what your clothing budget is for the month and for the year. This allows you to have realistic expectations when you are out shopping or when you need a new item for your wardrobe. If you're married, be sure to communicate this to your spouse. If you're living with your parents, discuss your needs with them.

MONDAY, DAY 23 TSN

Play with silhouette and shape. Try a voluminous palazzo pant, a full A-line skirt, a puff sleeve, a slim pant, a trumpet-hem skirt, or a cropped jacket.

TUESDAY, DAY 24 TSN

Add visual interest with layers. Try wearing a chambray shirt over a turtleneck, a belted duster sweater over a dress, a leather jacket over a faux fur vest, or a trench coat over a jumpsuit. Layering often makes a simple foundational piece look more sophisticated and intentional.

WEDNESDAY, DAY 25 WN

Wear your favorite (season-appropriate) scarf — and maybe even tie it up a new way.

THURSDAY, DAY 26 TSN

Try using a belt to add texture and structure to a long jacket, dress, sweater, or skirt.

FRIDAY, DAY 27 WN

Take something fancy and dress it down. Try a patent leather shoe with denim, a streamlined blazer with a simple tank, or a floral dress with a casual leather sandal.

SATURDAY, DAY 28 WCO

Go through your loungewear, pajamas, and workout clothes. Do you have thirty hoodies, stained spandex leggings, or mismatched loungewear? Bag them up and set them aside.

SUNDAY, DAY 29 SV

Take out your journal and record your takeaways from this #worthyofwearing challenge. What three things are you grateful for? Do you see yourself differently now, and if so, how?

MONDAY, DAY 30 WCO

Locate the clothing you bagged up. Decide what will get donated, resold, swapped with friends, and thrown away or recycled. Get rid of what's holding you back and move forward in your journey to fully clothing yourself as #worthyofwearing.

THIRTY-DAY ACTION PLAN

SUN	MON	TUE	WED	THU	FRI	SAT
01 S V	02 T S N	03 W N	04 T S N	05 W N	06 S V	07 W C O
08 S V	09 W N	10 S V	11 S V	12 W N	13 S V	14 W C O
15 S V	16 S V	17 T S N	18 S V	19 T S N	20 W N	21 W C O
22 S V	23 T S N	24 T S N	25 W N	26 T S N	27 W N	28 W C O
29 S V	30 W C O					

"'MANY ARE THE WOMEN OF PROVEN WORTH, BUT YOU HAVE EXCELLED THEM ALL.' CHARM IS DECEPTIVE AND BEAUTY FLEETING; THE WOMAN WHO FEARS THE LORD IS TO BE PRAISED. ACCLAIM HER FOR THE WORK OF HER HANDS, AND LET HER DEEDS PRAISE HER AT THE CITY GATES."

PROVERBS 31:29–31

A PRAYER

I ASK YOU, LORD, TO REMOVE ANY WALLS
AROUND MY HEART THAT PREVENT ME FROM
KNOWING HOW WORTHY I AM OF RECEIVING
AND SHARING YOUR LOVE. HELP ME TO BE A
LIGHT IN THIS WORLD WITH COURAGE AND
GRACE. O LORD, I ENTRUST TO YOU MY
VOCATION, MY TALENTS, AND THOSE I SERVE
DAILY IN MY MISSION. GUIDE ME, DEAR JESUS,
AND LET ALL OF MY ACHIEVEMENTS BE FOR
YOUR GLORY.

AMEN.

RESOURCES

See these resources and more at www.worthyofwearing.com/resources.

Personal development:

1. *StrengthsFinder 2.0* by Tom Rath / Gallup. Use the StrengthsFinder test to determine your God-given strengths.

2. The Catherine of Siena Institute's Called & Gifted Study for discerning your charisms and spiritual gifts to learn how you are called to serve the Kingdom of Christ on earth.

3. *Atomic Habits* by James Clear to learn how to make goals into habits in a very practical way.

4. *The Temperament God Gave You* by Art and Laraine Bennett to discover the characteristics, strengths, and pitfalls of your personality.

5. *The Gift of Imperfection* by Brené Brown to understand how perfectionism suffocates our mission.

Spirituality:

1. *The Heart of Perfection* by Colleen Carroll Campbell

2. *Remade for Happiness* by Fulton Sheen

3. *The Way of Trust and Love: A Retreat Guided by St. Thérèse of Lisieux* by Jacques Philippe

4. *The Reed of God* by Caryll Houselander

5. *God Is Love* by Pope Benedict XVI

6. *The Anti-Mary Exposed* by Dr. Carrie Gress

7. *The Privilege of Being a Woman* by Alice von Hildebrand

8. *The Other Side of Beauty* by Leah Darrow

Personal Style:

1. *The Curated Closet* by Anuschka Rees

2. *The Way She Wears It* by Dallas Shaw

3. *Living in Style* by Rachel Zoe

4. *Advanced Style* by Ari Seth Cohen

5. *Bill Cunningham: On the Street* by *The New York Times*

ACKNOWLEDGMENTS

Thank you . . .

To the Blessed Virgin Mary, who has revealed her closeness and maternal care to me in innumerable ways. While writing this book, I discovered that Pope St. John Paul the Great dedicated the year I was born, 1988, to Mary. I was baptized on the solemnity of the Immaculate Conception that same year. Every step of this journey, from the first email to the approval of the book's outline, occurred on a Marian feast day, which was most definitely not a coincidence.

To the women in the #worthyofwearing community who entrusted to me their personal stories of growth, joys, aha moments, and struggles. Your solidarity has inspired me and countless other women who have felt stuck, unseen, and unworthy. Thank you for joining me in this journey. Christ needs our light.

To Molly Rublee, John Barger, Anna Maria Dube, and the Sophia Institute Press team for believing in this message and working diligently to share it far and wide. Thank you, Molly Wierman, for your thorough edits that clarified and solidified this text. And many thanks to Tess Barber for the Aleteia article that got this ship sailing.

To my wise mentors who have been generous beyond measure with their time and encouragement: Glory Darbellay, Stephanie Weinert, Whitney Ray, Dr. Carrie Gress, Mary Lenaburg, and Leah Darrow.

To my sisters in Christ who are part of my story and whom I love so dearly, especially KP, Stephanie, the Kampa women, Tehri, Loretta, Allie, Jessie, Megan, Kristen, Kristin, Janet, Mary Kate, Janine, Jackie, Natalie, Bridget, and Aubry.

To the incredible photographer, designer, and art-director-in-chief Marquel Patton, who captured my vision and brought it to life. Thank goodness for that chance meeting at Cafe Gitane.

To Reagan Antonio, who worked tirelessly with me to plan the photo shoots, style models, organize accessories, and turn my brain dumps into beautiful Trello boards, all while trudging through the first trimester with your first babe. You are the hype girl every woman needs in her life.

To my lovely friends, the models who jumped into the project with enthusiasm on a hot September afternoon in Washington D. C., to show the world what modern Catholics look like: Adele, Ben, and their gorgeous Collins family; sisters Nneka and Ogechi Akalegbere; Cecilia Pappas; Caroline Ricardo; Sophie Wheeler and her unborn son; my mom, Gina Pelella; my daughter, Cecilia Caruso; Mary Lenaburg; Natalie Peters; Megan Philip and her darling Mariyam; Kathleen O'Beirne; Reagan Antonio; Fatima Perez and her unborn baby; Josephine von Dohlen; and my sister Alexandra Hieronymus and her unborn son. Big thanks to our hair-genius-in-residence Bethany Marzullo, who styled hair for our studio shoot and made us feel so pampered.

To my devoted husband, Stephen, and our dearest children; my parents, Mark and Gina; my sister, Ally, and her husband, Mark, with their children; my brother, Mark, and his lovely Jena; my brothers-in-law, Avery and Patrick; and Stephen's parents, Andy and Carol, who covered me with their prayers, sacrifices, encouragement, and care. I've never been prouder of our crazy family.

Worthy of Wearing came out of my thoughts and onto paper thanks to the helping hands of dear friends who rocked the baby, entertained littles, read all of our storybooks, made meals, encouraged my doubts, folded mountains of laundry, washed endless dishes, unpacked moving boxes, tidied messes, and fielded all the unknowns while I typed. Your belief in this movement is humbling, and I am better for having you in my life.

AMDG!

xox,
NMC

NOTES

1. Pope John Paul II, *Letter to Women* (June 29, 1995), no. 6.

2. Pope John Paul II, *Letter to Women,* no. 11.

3. Pope John Paul II, *Letter to Women,* no. 3.

4. St. Thérèse of Lisieux, *The Story of a Soul: The Autobiography of the Little Flower* (Charlotte, NC: TAN Books, 2010), 163.

5. Katie Little, "How Tony Robbins Rebounded from an Abusive Childhood to Create a Billion-Dollar Empire," CNBC, June

27, 2016, https://www.cnbc.com/2016/06/27/tony-robbins-from-an-abusive-childhood-to-a-billion-dollar-empire.html.

6. Pope John Paul II, Apostolic Letter *Mulieris Dignitatem* (On the Dignity and Vocation of Women) (August 15, 1988), no. 5.

7. Carrie Gress, *The Anti-Mary Exposed: Rescuing the Culture from Toxic Femininity* (Charlotte, NC: TAN Books, 2019), 151.

8. Pope Pius XI, "A Papal Decree Concerning Modesty" (January 12, 1930).

9. C. S. Lewis, *The Screwtape Letters* (New York: HarperCollins, 2009), chap. 2, Kindle.

10. Homily of His Holiness Benedict XVI, Lourdes, Rosary Square, September 13, 2008.

11. Francis Fernandez, *In Conversation with God: Meditations for Each Day of the Year*, vol. 5, *Ordinary Time: Weeks 24–34*

(New York: Scepter, 2005), 291–292.

12. Margaret Cardillo, *Just Being Audrey* (New York: HarperCollins, 2011).

13. Josemaría Escrivá, *Furrow* (New York: Scepter, 2002), chap. 5, no. 161.

Sophia Institute

Sophia Institute is a nonprofit institution that seeks to nurture the spiritual, moral, and cultural life of souls and to spread the Gospel of Christ in conformity with the authentic teachings of the Roman Catholic Church.

Sophia Institute Press fulfills this mission by offering translations, reprints, and new publications that afford readers a rich source of the enduring wisdom of mankind.

Sophia Institute also operates the popular online resource CatholicExchange.com. Catholic Exchange provides world news from a Catholic perspective as well as daily devotionals and articles that will help readers to grow in holiness and live a life consistent with the teachings of the Church.

In 2013, Sophia Institute launched Sophia Institute for Teachers to renew and rebuild Catholic culture through service to Catholic education. With the goal of nurturing the spiritual, moral, and cultural life of souls, and an abiding respect for the role and work of teachers, we strive to provide materials and programs that are at once enlightening to the mind and ennobling to the heart; faithful and complete, as well as useful and practical.

Sophia Institute gratefully recognizes the Solidarity Association for preserving and encouraging the growth of our apostolate over the course of many years. Without their generous and timely support, this book would not be in your hands.

www.SophiaInstitute.com
www.CatholicExchange.com
www.SophiaInstituteforTeachers.org

Sophia Institute Press ® is a registered trademark of Sophia Institute.
Sophia Institute is a tax-exempt institution as defined by the
Internal Revenue Code, Section 501(c)(3). Tax ID 22-2548708.